Multilingual Phrase Book

Nichole Haines

Copyright © 2023 by Nichole Haines

All rights reserved.

No portion of this book may be reproduced in any form without written permission from the publisher or author, except as permitted by U.S. copyright law.

Contents

1. Chapter 1 — 1
2. Multilingual Phrase Book — 2
3. Russian, German,Spanish, Ukrainian, and Polish — 3
4. Written By NicholeHaines — 4
5. ©2023 Nichole Haines — 5
6. Chapter 6 — 6
7. Chapter 7 — 8
8. Chapter 8 — 9
9. Chapter 9 — 12
10. Chapter 10 — 13
11. Chapter 11 — 21
12. Chapter 12 — 23
13. Chapter 13 — 25
14. Chapter 14 — 30
15. Chapter 15 — 34
16. Chapter 16 — 38
17. Chapter 17 — 39

18. Chapter 18 — 40
19. Chapter 19 — 49
20. Chapter 20 — 55
21. Chapter 21 — 58
22. Chapter 22 — 62
23. Chapter 23 — 66
24. Chapter 24 — 76
25. Chapter 25 — 77
26. Chapter 26 — 81
27. Chapter 27 — 84
28. Chapter 28 — 88
29. Chapter 29 — 91
30. Chapter 30 — 95
31. Chapter 31 — 97
32. Chapter 32 — 102
33. Chapter 33 — 108
34. Chapter 34 — 111
35. Chapter 35 — 117
36. Chapter 36 — 118
37. Chapter 37 — 122
38. Chapter 38 — 127
39. Chapter 39 — 134
40. Chapter 40 — 138
41. Chapter 41 — 141

42.	Chapter 42	142
43.	Chapter 43	143
44.	Chapter 44	144
45.	Chapter 45	151
46.	Chapter 46	155
47.	Chapter 47	160
48.	Chapter 48	164
49.	Chapter 49	171
50.	Chapter 50	173
51.	Chapter 51	178
52.	Chapter 52	179
53.	Chapter 53	180
54.	Chapter 54	181
55.	Chapter 55	182

Https://www.freepik.com/free-vector/realistic-colorful-rainbow-concept_7607090.htm#query=rainbow&from_query=rainbow%20cat&position=4&from_view=search&track=sph">Image by pikisuperstar</a> on Freepik

Multilingual Phrase Book

Chapter 3
Russian, German, Spanish, Ukrainian, and Polish

Written By
NicholeHaines

©2023 Nichole Haines

POLISH

1. She visits her father.   Ona Odwiedza ojca.
2. I call my friend.
Dzwonię do mojego przyjaciela.
3. I travel a lot.   Ja podróżuje duzo.

15. They drink water and juice. Piją wodę i sok.
16. You make Tea.   Robisz herbatę.
17. I drink water with ice. Ja piję wodę z lodem.
18. He would like black coffee.
On Chciałby czarnej kawy.

19. She would like milk.   Ona Chciałaby mleka.

20. I'm eating a sandwich. Jem kanapkę.

21. I'm eating a sandwich with cheese.
Jem kanapkę z serem.

22. I take a piece of bread.   Biorę kawałek chleba.

23. We take two pieces of cheese.
Bierzemy dwa kawałki sera.

24. Do you have fish?   Czy masz ryby?

25. Where is the salt?   Gdzie jest sól?

26. Can you bring me a fork?
Możesz mi przynieść widelec?

27. Can you bring me a spoon?
Możesz mi przynieść widelec?

28. Do you have a city map?   Czy masz mapę miasta?

29. Where is the post office?   Gdzie jest poczta?

30. Where is the pharmacy?   Gdzie jest poczta?

31. Where is the mall?   Gdzie jest centrum handlowe?

32. We need rice and bread.   Potrzebujemy ryżu i chleba.

33. We need tomatoes for the soup.   Do zupy potrzebujemy pomidorów.

34. Where is the grocery store?   Gdzie jest supermarket?

35. Where is the market?   Gdzie jest rynek?

36. Do you sell friuts and vegetables?   Czy Sprzedajesz owoce i warzywa.

37. We sell fruits and vegetables.   Zajmujemy się sprzedażą owoców i warzyw.

38. I have to buy a book.   Muszę kupić książkę.

39. I have to go to the bookstore.   Muszę iść do księgarni.

40. I have to go to the supermarket.   Muszę iść do supermarketu.

Image by <a href="https://www.freepik.com/free-vector/cart-with-blue-stripes-cotton-candy-background_1221930.htm#query=candy%20cars&position=9&from_view=search&track=ais">Freepik</a>

USEFUL POLISH PHRASES

1. Cześć! - Hello!
2. Dziękuję! - Thank you!
3. Przepraszam! - Excuse me!
4. Tak - Yes
5. Nie - No
6. Proszę - Please
7. Jak się masz? - How are you?
8. Nie rozumiem. - I don't understand.
9. Gdzie jest...? - Where is...?
10. Ile to kosztuje? - How much does this cost?
11. Mówię po angielsku. - I speak English.
12. Bardzo mi miło! - Nice to meet you!
13. Mam na imię... - My name is...
14. Nie rozumiem cię. - I don't understand you.
15. Pomóż mi, proszę. - Help me, please.
16. Jak masz na imię? - What is your name?
17. Jestem z... - I am from...
18. Dzień dobry! - Good day!
19. Przepraszam! - I'm sorry!
20. Do widzenia! - Goodbye!
21. Jestem wdzięczny/wdzięczna! - I am grateful!
22. Nie wiem. - I don't know.

23. Co robić? - What to do?
24. Czy mówisz po angielsku? - Do you speak English?
25. Jak mogę pomóc? - How can I help?
26. Gdzie jest toaleta? - Where is the toilet?
27. Jestem głodny/głodna. - I am hungry.
28. Chcę się napić. - I want to drink.
29. Jestem zmęczony/zmęczona. - I am tired.
30. Jestem szczęśliwy/szczęśliwa. - I am happy.
31. Dziękuję za wszystko. - Thank you for everything.
32. Kocham cię. - I love you.
33. Dzień dobry! - Good morning!
34. Dobry wieczór! - Good evening!
35. Słucham muzyki. - I am listening to music.
36. Oglądam telewizję. - I am watching TV.
37. Czytam książkę. - I am reading a book.
38. Idę do domu. - I am going home.
39. Gdzie mieszkasz? - Where do you live?
40. Jestem zajęty/zajęta. - I am busy.
41. Uczę się na uniwersytecie. - I study at the university.
42. Chcę odpocząć. - I want to relax.
43. Chcę spotkać się z przyjaciółmi. - I want to meet with friends.
44. Witamy! - Welcome!
45. Zrobiłem/zrobiłam się głodny/głodna. - I got hungry.
46. Jestem gotowy/gotowa. - I am ready.
47. Nie zgadzam się. - I disagree.
48. Zgadzam się. - I agree.
49. Do zobaczenia wkrótce! - See you soon!
50. Kocham to!
51. Gdzie jest biblioteka? - Where is the library?
52. Co to jest? - What is this?

53. Potrzebuję pomocy. - I need help.

54. Czy mogę prosić o wskazówki? - Can I ask for directions?

55. Jak dojechać do...? - How to get to...?

56. Czy mógłby Pan/Pani powtórzyć, proszę? - Could you repeat, please?

57. Czy jest tu gdzieś WiFi? - Is there any WiFi here?

58. Mogę prosić o menu? - Can I have the menu, please?

59. Mógłby Pan/Pani zrobić mi zdjęcie? - Could you take a picture of me, please?

60. Co polecasz do zwiedzania w okolicy? - What do you recommend to visit in the area?

61. Czy to jest bezpieczne? - Is it safe?

62. Czy tu są jakieś atrakcje w pobliżu? - Are there any attractions nearby?

63. Czy tu jest sklep spożywczy? - Is there a grocery store here?

64. Jak długo to potrwa? - How long will it take?

65. Czy jest jakiś dobry restauracja tutaj? - Is there a good restaurant here?

66. Czy możemy dostać rachunek? - Can we have the bill?

67. Czy masz jakieś wolne pokoje? - Do you have any vacancies?

68. Czy można płacić kartą kredytową? - Can I pay by credit card?

69. Gdzie mogę znaleźć autobus/metro? - Where can I find a bus/subway?

70. Czy można tu palić? - Is smoking allowed here?

71. Czy możesz mi pomóc? - Can you help me?

72. Czy to jest drogie? - Is it expensive?

73. Czy możesz to powtórzyć? - Can you repeat that?

74. Czy masz jakieś rekomendacje? - Do you have any recommendations?

Image by <a href="https://www.freepik.com/free-vector/cart-with-blue-stripes-cotton-candy-background_1221930.htm#query=candy%20cars&position=9&from_view=search&track=ais">Freepik</a>

USEFUL POLISH AIRPORT PHRASES

1. Czy mówisz po angielsku? (Chy moovish poh ang-yel-skoo?) - Do you speak English?

2. Proszę o informację (Pro-she uh in-for-mat-s-yun) - I need information.

3. Gdzie jest bramka numer sześć? (G-djeh yest bram-ka noo-mer shehsh?) - Where is gate number six?

4. Czy mógłby Pan pomóc mi z moim bagażem? (Chy moogw-bee Pan po-moots mee z moeem bag-az-em?) - Could you help me with my luggage, please?

5. Czy jest tu toaleta? (Chy yest tooa-let-a?) - Is there a restroom here?

6. Proszę o kawę (Pro-she uh ka-veh) - I would like a coffee, please.

7. Gdzie mogę znaleźć taksówkę? (G-djeh mo-geh znah-lehnts tahk-soof-keh?) - Where can I find a taxi?

8. Czy można pożyczyć ładowarkę do telefonu? (Chy pow-zheech woh-chich wah-doosh-char-koo do teh-le-fo-noo?) - Can I borrow a phone charger?

9. Czy są wolne miejsca w samolocie? (Chy saw vol-neh mye-sh-cha v sa-mo-lo-tsyeh?) - Are there any available seats on the flight?

10. Czy mogę zobaczyć rozkład lotów? (Chy mo-geh zoh-ba-cheech roz-klad lo-toof?) - Can I see the flight schedule?

11. Jak długo potrwa odprawa? (Yak woo-go pot-rva od-pra-va?) - How long will the check-in take?

12. Gdzie mogę odebrać swoje bagaże? (G-djeh mo-geh o-deh-bra-choh svo-ye ba-ga-zheh?) - Where can I collect my luggage?

13. Czy lot został opóźniony? (Chy lot zos-taw o-po-zhoh-nee-on-eh?) - Has the flight been delayed?

14. Czy mogę płacić kartą kredytową? (Chy mo-geh pwah-cheech kar-tam kreh-dy-to-vam?) - Can I pay with a credit card?

15. Czy mogę zamówić taksówkę? (Chy mo-geh za-mo-veesh tahk-soof-keh?) - Can I order a taxi?

16. Gdzie jest wyjście? (G-djeh yest vi-ysh-tye?) - Where is the exit?

17. Czy jest tu bezpłatne Wi-Fi? (Chy yest too be-shpwat-neh Wi-Fi?) - Is there free Wi-Fi here?

18. Czy mogę zobaczyć mój bilet? (Chy mo-geh zoh-ba-cheech moy bee-let?) - Can I see my ticket?

19. Czy możemy zmienić miejsce przy oknie? (Chy mo-zhe-meh zmye-nich mye-ye-sh-ch-eh pree ok-n-eh?) - Can we change seats near the window?

20. Gdzie jest punkt informacyjny? (G-djeh yest poont in-for-mat-see-yon-ny?) - Where is the information desk?

21. Czy mogę zobaczyć paszport? (Chy mo-geh zoh-ba-cheech pash-port?) - Can I see your passport?

22. Czy mogę skorzystać z toalety? (Chy mo-geh skor-zhi-stash toa-let-y?) - May I use the restroom?

23. Czy torebka może być używana jako bagaż podręczny? (Chy toh-reh-bka mo-zheh bych oo-zhee-wa-na ya-ko ba-gaz po-dren-ni?) - Can this purse be used as carry-on luggage?

24. Gdzie jest strefa odprawy? (G-djeh yest stref-a od-pra-vy?) - Where is the check-in area?

25. Czy mogę zarezerwować miejsce przy oknie? (Chy mo-geh za-re-ze-rvo-vach mye-ye-sh-ch-eh pree ok-n-eh?) - Can I reserve a window seat?

26. Czy toaleta jest dostępna dla niepełnosprawnych? (Chy toa-let-a yest dost-ep-na dla nyeh-pe-won-sprowvnch?) - Is the restroom accessible for people with disabilities?

27. Czy jest tu restauracja? (Chy yest too re-stau-ra-tsy-ah?) - Is there a restaurant here?

28. Gdzie jest poczekalnia? (G-djeh yest poh-chez-kal-nyah?) - Where is the waiting area?

29. Czy pracują tutaj lekarze? (Chy pra-choo too-taj le-kar-zeh?) - Are there doctors working here?

30. Czy mogę zmienić walutę? (Chy mo-geh zmye-nich wah-loo-ta?) - Can I exchange currency?

31. Czy jest tu bankomat? (Chy yest too ban-ko-mat?) - Is there an ATM here?

32. Czy możemy się zameldować? (Chy mo-zhe-meh syeh za-mel-do-vach?) - Can we check-in?

33. Gdzie mogę kupić bilet na autobus? (G-djeh mo-ghe koop-yich bee-let na ow-to-boos?) - Where can I buy a bus ticket?

34. Czy mogę zarezerwować miejsce dla niemowlęcia? (Chy mo-geh za-re-ze-rvo-vatch mye-ye-sh-cheh dla nyem-ow-len-tsyah?) - Can I reserve a seat for an infant?

35. Czy jest tu bezpieczne przechowalnie bagażu? (Chy yest too be-shpyetch-nyeh pr-eh-cho-va-lyeh-ba-gazh-oo?) - Is there a secure luggage storage here?

36. Czy mogę zobaczyć plan lotniska? (Chy mo-geh zoh-ba-cheech plan lo-tnis-ka?) - Can I see the airport map?

37. Czy lot ma przekąski na pokładzie? (Chy lot ma psheh-kon-skee na pok-wad-zh-eh?) - Does the flight have snacks on board?

38. Gdzie jest strefa odbioru bagażu? (G-djeh yest stref-a od-bee-oo-roo ba-ga-zh-oo?) - Where is the baggage claim area?

39. Czy można podłączyć się do Wi-Fi? (Chy pow-zhoh-nach po-dwoo-chee-seh do Wi-Fi?) - Can I connect to the Wi-Fi?

40. Czy mogę zarezerwować miejsce dla osoby niepalącej? (Chy mo-geh za-re-ze-rvo-vach mye-ye-sh-cheh dla oh-so-bee nyeh-pa-won-tsy?) - Can I reserve a seat for a non-smoker?

41. Gdzie znajduje się sala VIP? (G-djeh zna-yoo-yeh sye sa-la VIP?) - Where is the VIP lounge?

42. Czy mogę skorzystać z komputera? (Chy mo-geh skor-zhi-stach z kom-put-era?) - May I use the computer?

43. Czy jest tu sklep wolnocłowy? (Chy yest too sklep vol-no-cho-vy?) - Is there a duty-free shop here?

44. Czy mogę zarezerwować wynajem samochodu? (Chy mo-geh za-re-ze-rvo-vach vi-nyem sa-mo-ho-do?) - Can I make a car rental reservation?

45. Gdzie jest biuro informacji turystycznej? (G-djeh yest byoo-ro in-for-ma-ts-ee too-rist-yeh-nyeh?) - Where is the tourist information office?

46. Czy mogę zmienić miejsce dla osoby o ograniczonej mobilności? (Chy mo-geh zmye-nich mye-ye-sh-cheh dla oh-so-be o og-ra-nee-ch-oh-neh mo-bil-nos-chee?) - Can I change seats for a person with reduced mobility?

47. Czy jest tu sala konferencyjna? (Chy yest too sa-la kon-fe-ren-tsyj-na?) - Is there a conference room here?

48. Czy mogę kupić gazetę? (Chy mo-geh koop-yich ga-zeh-teh?) - Can I buy a newspaper?

49. Czy jest tu automat do biletów? (Chy yest too a-oo-to-mat do bee-let-oof?) - Is there a ticket vending machine here?

50. Dziękuję za pomoc! (Jen-koo-yoo za ho-mots!) - Thank you for your helpe

USEFUL POLISH BUSINESS PHRASES

1. Dzień dobry (jen DOH-bri) - Good morning/afternoon.

2. Czy mógłby pan/pani mi pomóc? (chi MOOHL-bi pan/pani mee poh-MOCH) - Could you help me, please?

3. Proszę (PRO-sheh) - Please.

4. Dziękuję (dyen-KOO-yeh) - Thank you.

5. Przepraszam (psheh-PRAH-sham) - I'm sorry/excuse me.

6. Jak się pan/pani ma? (Yak syeh pan/pani mah) - How are you?

7. Bardzo dobrze, dziękuję. (BAR-dzoh DOH-bzheh, dyen-KOO-yeh) - Very well, thank you.

8. Pomoże mi pan/pani? (poh-MOH-zheh mee pan/pani) - Can you help me?

9. Mam pytanie. (mam PEE-tah-nyeh) - I have a question.

10. Czy mogę umówić się na spotkanie? (chi MOH-geh oo-MO-veech syeh na spot-KAH-nyeh) - May I schedule a meeting?

11. Prześlij mi to emailem. (psheh-SHLEEM mee toh eh-MY-lem) - Send it to me by email.

12. Czy jesteś zainteresowany/zainteresowana ofertą? (chi YEHS-tesh zynteh-reh-SOH-van/zainteh-reh-SOH-vah-na oh-FER-tah) - Are you interested in the offer?

13. Czy możemy omówić szczegóły? (chi MOH-zheh-meh oh-MOO-vich SCHCHE-go-wee) - Can we discuss the details?

14. Mam pewne wątpliwości. (mam PEH-vneh VUHM-pli-voh-sci) - I have some doubts.

15. Czy są jakieś dodatkowe koszty? (chi sah YA-kyesh doh-DAH-koh-veh KOH-shtih) - Are there any additional costs?

16. Daj mi znać. (dai mee znahtch) - Let me know.

17. Czy mogę prosić o fakturę? (chi MOH-geh PRO-seesh oh FAHK-too-reh) - Can I ask for an invoice?

18. Nie ma sprawy. (Nye mah SPRAH-vi) - No problem.

19. Jestem zainteresowany/zainteresowana współpracą. (YES-tem zynteh-reh-SOH-van/zainteh-reh-SOH-vah-na vspoo-WRAH-tsah) - I am interested in cooperation.

20. Czy to jest dostępne? (chi toh yest doh-STEN-ve) - Is it available?

21. Chciałbym/chciałabym zamówić. (HCHAU-bim/hCHAU-bam za-MOV-ishch) - I would like to order.

22. Daj mi chwilę, proszę. (dai mee HVEE-leh, PRO-sheh) - Give me a moment, please.

23. Czy mogę zobaczyć ofertę? (chi MOH-geh zoh-BAH-cheech oh-FER-teh) - Can I see the offer?

24. Jakie są warunki płatności? (YAH-kyeh sah vah-RON-kee PWAT-no-sci) - What are the payment terms?

25. Jakie są korzyści? (YAH-kyeh sah koh-ZI-shchee) - What are the benefits?

26. Muszę to przemyśleć. (MOOSH-eh toh psheh-MI-shletch) - I need to think about it.

27. Czy mogę zapytać o termin realizacji? (chi MOH-geh za-PIT-ah o TEH-min rea-li-ZA-tsi) - Can I ask about the deadline?

28. Czy mogę liczyć na rabat? (chi MOH-geh LEE-choo na RAH-bat) - Can I expect a discount?

29. To jest za drogie. (toh yest za DROH-gyeh) - It's too expensive.

30. Gdzie mogę podpisać umowę? (gdzyeh MOH-geh pod-PEE-sach oo-MO-ve) - Where can I sign the contract?

31. Niestety, nie jestem zainteresowany/zainteresowana. (nyeh-STEH, nye YES-tem zynteh-re-SOH-van/zainteh-re-SOH-vah-na) - Unfortunately, I'm not interested.

32. Czy mogę skorzystać z toalety? (chi MOH-geh skor-ZIS-tahch stos-WAH-conscious Z toah-LEH-tih) - Can I use the restroom?

33. Dlaczego to jest takie ważne? (DLAH-cheh-go toh yest TAH-kyeh VAH-shne) - Why is it so important?

34. Czy jest możliwość negocjacji? (chi yest mozh-lee-VOSH nei-go-tsia-TSI) - Is there a possibility of negotiation?

35. Czy mogę dostać informacje na piśmie? (chi MOH-geh DOS-tahch in-for-MA-tsi-ye na PEE-shmye) - Can I have the information in writing?

36. Czy mogę odebrać zamówienie osobiście? (chi MOH-geh oh-DEB-rach za-MOV-yeh-nyeh oh-SO-beesh-che) - Can I collect the order personally?

37. Czy wszystko jest w porządku? (chi vshih-STKO yest v poh-ZHON-du) - Is everything all right?

38. Czy to jest możliwe do zrealizowania? (chi toh yest mozh-LEE-veh do zre-a-li-zo-WA-nia) - Is it possible to accomplish?

39. Właśnie o tym myślałem/myślałam. (VWA-shneh o tihm mihsh-LA-lem/mihsh-LA-vam) - I was just thinking about it.

40. Czy mogę prosić o dodatkowe informacje? (chi MOH-geh PRO-seesh oh doh-DAH-koh-veh in-for-MA-tsi-ye) - Can I ask for additional information?

41. Potrzebuję więcej czasu. (potsh-NEH-boo-yeh moreh chah-SOO) - I need more time.

42. Czy mogę coś zaproponować? (chi MOH-geh chosh za-pro-PO-no-vach) - Can I propose something?

43. To brzmi dobrze. (toh bzh-mee DOH-bzhe) - That sounds good.

44. Czy możemy to zrobić online? (chi MOH-zheh-meh toh ZROH-beech on-lin-eh) - Can we do it online?

45. Czy dostępne są jakieś zniżki? (chi doh-STEN-ve sah YA-kyesh zNEE-zh-ki) - Are there any discounts available?

46. To jest świetna oferta. (toh yest shvieht-nah oh-FER-tah) - It's a great offer.

47. Czy możemy to omówić jutro? (chi MOH-zheh-meh toh oh-MOO-vich YOO-troh) - Can we discuss it tomorrow?

48. Nie jestem pewien/pewna. (nyeh YES-tem PEH-vee-yen/PEH-vna) - I'm not sure.

49. Będę musiał/będę musiała to przemyśleć. (BEN-deh MOO-shau/moo-SWAU toh pshem-I-shletch) - I'll have to think about it.

50. Czy mogę zobaczyć portfolio? (chi MOH-geh zoh-BAH-cheech por-FO-lyoh) - Can I see the portfolio?

1. Czy mogę prosić o informację? (Chy moh-geh pro-seeć o in-for-ma-cyeh?) - Can I ask for information?

2. Gdzie jest bramka numer...? (Gd-zie jest brahm-kah nu-mer...) - Where is gate number...?

3. Czy to jest terminal międzynarodowy? (Chy to yest ter-mee-nal myen-dzi-na-ro-do-vi?) - Is this the international terminal?

4. Czy wystawiają paszporty? (Chy wy-sta-vya-yon pasz-por-ty?) - Do they issue passports?

5. Czy mogę wynająć samochód na lotnisku? (Chy mo-geh wi-na-yont sa-mo-hoot na lot-ni-sku?) - Can I rent a car at the airport?

6. Które drzwi są przylotów? (Ktoo-reh drz-vee sah przy-lot-oof?) - Which doors are for arrivals?

7. Które drzwi są odlotów? (Ktoo-reh drz-vee sah od-lot-oof?) - Which doors are for departures?

8. Czy jest bezpieczne zostawić bagaż? (Chy yest bez-pyech-neh zo-sta-vish ba-gash?) - Is it safe to leave luggage?

9. Gdzie jest toaleta? (Gd-zie yest to-ah-le-ta?) - Where is the restroom?

10. Czy terminal ma Wi-Fi? (Chy ter-mee-nal ma Wi-Fi?) - Does the terminal have Wi-Fi?

11. Jak długo potrwa przelot? (Yak woon-go pot-rva pzelot?) - How long will the flight take?

12. Czy są opóźnienia? (Chy son o-poo-znyeh-ah?) - Are there any delays?

13. Czy muszę się zameldować? (Chy moos-esh shyah za-mel-do-vac?) - Do I need to check-in?

14. Gdzie mogę kupić bilet? (Gd-zie mo-geh koo-peech bee-let?) - Where can I buy a ticket?

15. Czy jest jakiś bank w pobliżu? (Chy yest yah-keesh bank v poh-blee-zhoo?) - Is there a bank nearby?

16. Czy jest punkt informacyjny? (Chy yest poont in-for-ma-tsy-oh-ny?) - Is there an information point?

17. Czy mogę użyć karty kredytowej? (Chy mo-geh oo-zheech kar-ti kre-dee-to-vey?) - Can I use a credit card?

18. Czy jest sklep wolnocłowy? (Chy yest sklep vol-no-clow-vi?) - Is there a duty-free shop?

19. Czy mają transport pomiędzy terminalami? (Chy ma-yont trans-port po-myen-dzi ter-mee-na-la-mi?) - Do they have transportation between terminals?

20. Czy jest dostęp dla osób niepełnosprawnych? (Chy yest dos-typ dla o-soomb nye-peł-no-sprav-nih?)

Image by <a href="https://www.freepik.com/free-vector/cart-with-blue-stripes-cotton-candy-background_1221930.htm#query=candy%20cars&position=9&from_view=search&track=ais">Freepik</a>

NUMBERS IN POLISH

- jeden (yed-den)

2 - dwa (d-vah)

3 - trzy (t-zih)

4 - cztery (ch-te-re)

5 - pięć (pyehnch)

6 - sześć (sheh-shch)

7 - siedem (syeh-dem)

8 - osiem (oh-syem)

9 - dziewięć (dyeh-vyehnch)

10 - dziesięć (dzye-shch)

11 - jedenaście (yed-den-ah-sheh)

12 - dwanaście (dva-nah-sheh)

13 - trzynaście (t-zhi-nah-sheh)
14 - czternaście (ch-te-rnah-sheh)
15 - piętnaście (pyehn-chah-sheh)
16 - szesnaście (sheh-snah-sheh)
17 - siedemnaście (syed-em-nah-sheh)
18 - osiemnaście (oh-syem-nah-sheh)
19 - dziewiętnaście (dyev-yen-nah-sheh)
20 - dwadzieścia (dva-dyeh-sh-chah)
21 - dwadzieścia jeden (dva-dyeh-sh-chah yed-den)
22 - dwadzieścia dwa (dva-dyeh-sh-chah d-vah)
23 - dwadzieścia trzy (dva-dyeh-sh-chah t-zih)
...
100 - sto (stoh)

Image by <a href="https://www.freepik.com/free-vector/cart-with-blue-stripes-cotton-candy-background_1221930.htm#query=candy%20cars&position=9&from_view=search&track=ais">Freepik</a>

1. Cześć! (cheshch) - Hello!

2. Dzień dobry! (dyen dob-ri) - Good day!

3. Przepraszam, czy mogę rozmawiać z...? (pshe-prah-sham, chi mo-geh roz-mah-vyahch z...) - Excuse me, may I speak with...?

4. Jestem zainteresowany/zainteresowana informacją na temat... (yes-tem zyn-te-re-so-wah-nuh in-for-ma-cyam na te-mat...) - I am interested in information about...

5. Czy mogę zostawić wiadomość? (chi mo-geh zoh-stah-veech vyah-do-moshch) - Can I leave a message?

6. Proszę zaczekać chwilę. (pro-sheh zah-cheh-kachh chi-leh) - Please wait a moment.

7. Czy mógłby Pan/Pani powtórzyć? (chi moog-wee pan/pani pov-too-rzich) - Could you repeat, please?

8. Na jakiej linii się znajduję? (na ya-keh lee-nee syeh zna-yoo-yoo) - Which line am I on?

9. Przepraszam, mogę połączyć z innym numerem? (pshe-prah-sham, mo-geh poo-wa-chich z een-nim noo-me-rem) - I'm sorry, can I connect to another number?

10. Czy mogę zamówić usługę telefoniczną? (chi mo-geh za-moo-veech oo-swoo-geh te-le-fo-neech-nah) - Can I request a telephone service?

11. Czy mają Państwo usługę obsługi klienta? (chi ma-yon panst-vo oo-swoo-geh ob-swoo-gee klen-tah) - Do you have customer service?

12. Który numer powinienem wybrać? (kto-ri noo-mer po-shi-ne-m vee-brach) - Which number should I dial?

13. Ile kosztuje ta rozmowa? (ee-leh ko-shoo-tyeh tah roz-mo-va) - How much does this call cost?

14. Czy akceptują Państwo płatności kartą? (chi a-k-cept-oo-yon panstvo pwat-en-chee kar-tam) - Do you accept card payments?

15. Czy mogę przekazać wiadomość telefoniczną? (chi mo-geh pshe-ka-zach vyah-do-mooshch te-le-fo-neech-nah) - Can I leave a telephone message?

16. Chciałbym umówić się na spotkanie. (h-chya-wim oo-moo-vich syeh na spot-ka-nyeh) - I would like to make an appointment.

17. Dzwonię w sprawie mojego zamówienia. (dzwon-yeh v spra-vye mo-yeh-go za-moo-vyen-ya) - I'm calling about my order.

18. Czy może mi Pan/Pani pomóc? (chi mo-zheh mee pan/pani po-mooch) - Can you help me, please?

19. Chciałbym zareklamować produkt/usługę. (h-chya-wim za-re-kla-mo-vach pro-doost/oos-woo-geh) - I would like to complain about a product/service.

20. Czy mógłby Pan/Pani oddzwonić później? (chi moog-wee pan/pani od-dzvo-neech poo-zh-ney) - Could you call me back later?

21. Przepraszam, nie mogę usłyszeć dobrze. (pshe-prah-sham, nyeh mo-geh oo-si-shech do-brzech) - I'm sorry, I can't hear you well.

22. Czy mogę ustawić przekierowanie? (chi mo-geh oos-ta-vich pshe-kye-ro-va-neh) - Can I set up call forwarding?

23. Czy mogę zmienić numer PIN? (chi mo-geh zmye-nych noo-mer pin) - Can I change my PIN number?

24. Potrzebuję informacji na temat roamingu. (po-tseh-boo-yeh in-for-ma-tsee na te-mat ro-a-min-goo) - I need information about roaming.

25. Czy operator obsługuje język angielski? (chi op-rah-tor ob-sloo-goo-yeh yen-zhik an-gyels-ki) - Does the operator speak English?

26. Dziękuję za pomoc. (jen-koo-yeh za ho-mots) - Thank you for your help.

27. Czy mogę odebrać wiadomość głosową? (chi mo-geh o-de-brahch vyah-do-mooshch gwo-so-vah) - Can I retrieve my voice message?

28. Przepraszam, źle wybrałem numer. (pshe-prah-sham, zhle vee-brah-wem noo-mer) - Sorry, I dialed the wrong number.

29. Czy mogę rozłączyć połączenie? (chi mo-geh roz-lon-cheech poo-wa-chen-ye) - Can I hang up the call?

30. Czy mogę sprawdzić swoją pocztę głosową? (chi mo-geh sprav-jeech svo-ya po-chte glyo-so-vah) - Can I check my voicemail?

31. Czy są jakieś problemy z siecią? (chi sah ya-kyesh pro-ble-miy z syen-tsyam) - Are there any network issues?

32. Bardzo dziękuję za szybką odpowiedź. (bar-dzo jen-koo-yeh za shib-koo on-po-vy-esh) - Thank you very much for the prompt response.

33. Chciałem/chciałam się umówić na wizytę. (h-chya-wem/h-chya-wam syeh oo-moo-veech na vee-zee-te) - I wanted to make an appointment.

34. Czy mogę skorzystać z usługi przekierowania? (chi mo-geh skor-zyst-ash oos-woo-gee pshe-kye-ro-va-nee-ya) - Can I use the call forwarding service?

35. Niestety, musimy zakończyć rozmowę. (nyesy-teh, moo-si-mi za-ko-ntshee-tch roz-mo-ve) - Unfortunately, we have to end the call.

36. Czy mogę porozmawiać z menedżerem? (chi mo-geh po-roz-ma-vyahch z me-ne-dzhe-rem) - Can I speak with the manager?

37. Proszę o połączenie z działem obsługi klienta. (pro-sheh o poo-wa-chen-ye z dyah-lem ob-swoo-gee klen-ta) - Please connect me to customer service.

38. Czy mogę sprawdzić stan konta? (chi mo-geh sprav-jeech stan kon-ta) - Can I check my account balance?

39. Proszę o numer telefonu do firmy... (pro-sheh o nu-mer te-le-fo-noo do fir-mi) - Please give me the telephone number for...

40. Czy mogę anulować/odwołać rezerwację? (chi mo-geh a-nu-loo-vach/od-vo-wach re-zeer-va-tsyon) - Can I cancel a reservation?

41. Dziękuję za wyjaśnienie. (jen-koo-yeh za wi-ya-shne-nye) - Thank you for the explanation.

42. Czy mogę zarezerwować stolik w restauracji? (chi mo-geh za-re-zeer-vo-vach sto-leek v res-tau-ra-tsyi) - Can I book a table at the restaurant?

43. Czy mogę zmienić plan taryfowy? (chi mo-geh zmye-nych plan ta-ri-fo-vih) - Can I change my tariff plan?

44. Proszę o informacje na temat opłat roamingowych. (pro-sheh o in-for-ma-tsyo-neh na te-mat op-lat ro-a-min-gov-ikh) - Please provide information about roaming charges.

45. Czy mogę uzyskać fakturę? (chi mo-geh oo-zi-shech fak-too-re) - Can I get an invoice?

46. Czy obowiązuje jakaś umowa? (chi o-bo-vee-zoo-yeh ya-kash o-mo-va) - Is there any agreement in place?

47. Przepraszam, ale nie mogę rozpoznać głosu. (pshe-prah-sham, ah-leh nyeh mo-geh roz-poz-na-ch glyo-su) - I'm sorry, but I can't recognize the voice.

48. Czy mogę zmienić język w systemie telefonicznym? (chi mo-geh zmye-nych yen-zhik v sis-te-meh te-le-fo-neech-nim) - Can I change the language in the phone system?

49. Dziękuję za miłą rozmowę. (jen-koo-yeh za mee-wah roz-mo-ve) - Thank you for the nice conversation.

50. Czy mogę zwiększyć limit danych? (chi mo-geh zvee-eks-eech lee-mit da-neh) - Can I increase my data limit?

Image by <a href="https://www.freepik.com/free-photo/lollipops-sweets-popcorn-bag_6399056.htm#query=holiday%20candy&position=29&from_view=search&track=ais">Freepik</a>

USEFUL HOLIDAY PHRASES

1. Wesołych Świąt! (ve-soh-wih she-fyant) - Merry Christmas!

2. Szczęśliwego Nowego Roku! (shchen-swi-vo no-veh-go ro-koo) - Happy New Year!

3. Wesołych Świąt Bożego Narodzenia! (ve-soh-wih she-fyant bo-zhe-go na-ro-dze-nya) - Merry Christmas!

4. Szczęśliwej Zabawy Sylwestrowej! (shchen-swi-veh zab-ah-vih sil-ves-tro-veh) - Happy New Year's Eve party!

5. Sto lat! (sto laht) - A hundred years! (used to wish someone a long and healthy life)

6. Szczęść Boże! (shchen-shch bo-zhe) - God bless you!

7. Powodzenia! (po-vo-den-ya) - Good luck!

8. Szczęśliwej podróży! (shchen-swi-veh po-droo-zhi) - Have a nice trip!

9. Zdrowia i radości! (zdroh-vya ee ra-doi-shee) - Health and happiness!

10. Wielkanocne życzenia! (vyel-ka-noh-tchna zhi-chen-ya) - Easter wishes!

11. Spędź cudowny czas z rodziną! (spen-j choo-dov-ni tash z roh-dee-nah) - Have a wonderful time with family!

12. Zrób sobie przerwę i zrelaksuj się! (zrohb soh-byeh pshe-rveh ee zre-la-koo-y se) - Take a break and relax!

13. Ciesz się świętami! (cheesh sye she-vyen-tah-mee) - Enjoy the holidays!

14. Smacznego! (smach-neh-go) - Enjoy your meal!

15. Wesołego Alleluja! (ve-soh-weh-go al-le-loo-ya) - Happy Easter!

16. Miłego odpoczynku! (mee-weh-go o-dpo-chin-koo) - Have a nice rest!

17. Udanych zakupów! (oo-dan-yh za-ko-poof) - Successful shopping!

18. Piękne prezenty! (pyenk-neh prez-ent-y) - Beautiful gifts!

19. Wyjątkowego czasu z najbliższymi! (vya-yont-ko-veh tash-zoo nai-bleesh-shimi) - Special time with loved ones!

20. Radosnych chwil! (ra-dosh-nyh chveel) - Joyful moments!

21. Zrelaksuj się i baw dobrze! (zre-lak-sooy se ee bav do-bzhe) - Relax and have fun!

22. Pamiętaj o czasie dla siebie! (pa-myen-tai o cha-see dla sye-byeh) - Remember to have some time for yourself!

23. Radosnego świętowania! (ra-do-sne-go she-vyen-to-vah-nya) - Joyful celebration!

24. Gorących rozmów przy stole! (go-roh-hych roz-moof pshi stoh-leh) - Warm conversations at the table!

25. Cudownych wspomnień! (choo-dov-nih vspo-mnyen) - Wonderful memories!

26. Niech spełnią się Twoje marzenia! (nyeh speh-nya sye to-ye ma-rzhe-na) - May your dreams come true!

27. Niech radość wypełni Twoje życie! (nyeh ra-dosht vi-pyen-nee to-ye zhi-che) - May joy fill your life!

28. Pogody ducha! (po-go-di doo-ha) - Peace of mind!

29. Uśmiechaj się często! (oosh-mie-hai sye chesh-to) - Smile often!

30. Zbieraj piękne chwile! (zbyeh-rai pyenk-neh chvee-le) - Collect beautiful moments!

31. Cieszyć się zimowymi atrakcjami! (chee-shchich sye zee-mo-vi-mi a-trak-cha-mee) - Enjoy winter attractions!

32. Szczęśliwego wieczoru! (shchen-swi-vo vyeh-cho-roo) - Happy evening!

33. Wesołego Dnia Kobiet! (ve-soh-weh-go dnya ko-byet) - Happy Women's Day!

34. Radosnego śpiewania kolęd! (ra-do-sne-go shpvee-va-nya ko-lent) - Joyful carol singing!

35. Udanej imprezy sylwestrowej! (oo-da-ney im-preh-zih sil-ves-tro-veh) - Have a great New Year's party!

36. Miłego wieczoru wigilijnego! (mee-weh-go vyeh-cho-roo vi-gi-leey-neh-go) - Have a lovely Christmas Eve!

37. Odpoczynku na łonie natury! (o-dpo-chin-koo na wo-neh na-too-ri) - Relaxation in the lap of nature!

38. Orzeźwiających wakacji! (o-rze-shvi-ya-yon-yh va-ka-ts-yee) - Refreshing vacation!

39. Pięknych światełek świątecznych! (pyenk-nih she-vya-tek shvyan-teh-chnih) - Beautiful Christmas lights!

40. Zdrowych i spokojnych świąt! (zdro-vo-hih ee spo-ko-y-nyh she-vyaht) - Healthy and peaceful holidays!

41. Miłych spotkań z przyjaciółmi! (mee-lyh spot-kan z pshi-yat-choo-wmee) - Pleasant meetings with friends!

42. Radosnego ferii zimowych! (ra-do-sne-go fye-ree zee-mo-vih) - Joyful winter break!

43. Udanego odpoczynku na plaży! (oo-da-neh-go o-dpo-chin-koo na pla-zhi) - Have a great beach holiday!

44. Miłego wieczoru sylwestrowego! (mee-weh-go vyeh-cho-roo sil-ves-tro-veh-go) - Have a pleasant New Year's Eve!

45. Wesołej zabawy na karnawale! (ve-soh-lei za-bav-ih na kar-na-va-leh) - Enjoy the carnival party!

46. Życzę słonecznej pogody! (zhich-eh swo-neh-chnei po-go-dih) - I wish you sunny weather!

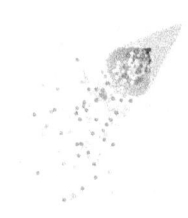

Image by <a href="https://www.freepik.com/free-photo/lollipops-sweets-popcorn-bag_6399056.htm#query=holiday%20candy&position=29&from_view=search&track=ais">Freepik</a>

USEFUL WEATHER POLISH PHRASES

1. Jaka jest pogoda dzisiaj? (yah-kah yest po-go-dah dzee-syahy) - What's the weather like today?

2. Czy będzie padać dzisiaj? (chi ben-dzhe pah-dahtz dzee-syahy) - Will it rain today?

3. Czy jest zimno? (chi yest zim-no) - Is it cold?

4. Czy jest ciepło? (chi yest chyep-wo) - Is it warm?

5. Czy jest wietrznie? (chi yest vyet-zhnie) - Is it windy?

6. Czy jest słonecznie? (chi yest swo-neh-chne) - Is it sunny?

7. Czy jest pochmurno? (chi yest poch-moor-no) - Is it cloudy?

8. Czy jest burzowo? (chi yest boor-zo-vo) - Is it stormy?

9. Czy jest mgła? (chi yest m-gwah) - Is it foggy?

10. Czy jest deszczowo? (chi yest desh-cho-vo) - Is it rainy?

11. Czy jest śnieg? (chi yest shnyek) - Is it snowing?

12. Jakie są temperatury? (yah-kyeh sahem-peh-roo-ri) - What are the temperatures?

13. Jest 20 stopni. (yest dvyen-tsye stoh-pnee) - It's 20 degrees.

14. Jest bardzo zimno. (yest bar-dzo zim-no) - It's very cold.

15. Jest przyjemnie ciepło. (yest pshi-yem-nyeh chyep-wo) - It's pleasantly warm.

16. Jest silny wiatr. (yest sil-ny vyat-r) - It's windy.

17. Jest pięknie słonecznie. (yest pyenk-nye swo-neh-chne) - It's beautifully sunny.

18. Jest pochmurnie i zimno. (yest poch-moor-nye ee zim-no) - It's cloudy and cold.

19. Jest burzowo i deszczowo. (yest boor-zo-vo ee desh-cho-vo) - It's stormy and rainy.

20. Jest mgła i mokro. (yest m-gwah ee mokro) - It's foggy and wet.

21. Spodziewaj się opadów. (spod-zhe-vai sye o-pah-doof) - Expect precipitation.

22. Będzie padać przez cały dzień. (ben-dyeh pah-dahts dzhez cha-weh dee-eyn) - It will rain all day.

23. Będzie padał śnieg wieczorem. (ben-dyeh pah-dau shnyek vyeh-cho-rem) - It will snow in the evening.

24. Prognoza na jutro mówi o burzach. (prog-no-za na yoo-tro moo-vee o boor-zah) - Tomorrow's forecast predicts storms.

25. Pogoda się poprawia. (po-go-dah syeh pop-ra-vee-ah) - The weather is getting better.

26. Pogoda jest stabilna. (po-go-dah yest sta-beel-na) - The weather is stable.

27. Słońce świeci przez cały dzień. (swohn-tsse shvyechi pshes cha-weh dee-eyn) - The sun is shining all day.

28. Jest silne zachmurzenie. (yest sil-neh zahkh-moo-zhe-nyeh) - It's heavily overcast.

29. Wieje silny wiatr. (vyeh-ye sil-ny vyat-r) - There's a strong wind blowing.

30. Mamy szansę na błękitne niebo. (ma-mi shan-seh na bwenk-tee-neh nyeh-bo) - We have a chance for clear skies.

31. Ostrzeżenie przed burzami. (os-tzhezh-nye-nye pred boor-za-mee) - Warning of storms.

32. Deszcz utrudnia poruszanie się po mieście. (desh-chootz oo-trood-nya po-roo-sha-nyeh-nye syeh po myesht-se) - Rain makes it difficult to move around the city.

33. Śnieg utworzył warstwę lodu na drodze. (shnyeg oo-tvo-reel var-stve lo-doo na drod-ze) - Snow has formed an ice layer on the road.

34. Pogoda się psuje. (po-go-dah syeh psoo-yeh) - The weather is getting worse.

35. Duże zachmurzenie może przynieść burze. (doo-zhe zahkh-moo-zen-yeh mo-tseh pshy-nesht boor-zeh) - Heavy cloud cover may bring storms.

36. Temperatura powoli wzrasta. (tem-peh-ra-too-ra po-vo-lee vzhah-sta) - The temperature is slowly rising.

37. Na niebie pojawiły się tęczowe chmurki. (na nyeh-byeh po-ya-vee-woo si-eh ten-chov-veh hmoor-kee) - Rainbow-colored clouds have appeared in the sky.

38. Rankiem będzie rosa. (ran-kyem ben-dyeh ro-sah) - There will be dew in the morning.

39. Mamy piękne letnie dni. (ma-mi pyenk-neh let-nyeh dnee) - We have beautiful summer days.

40. Wieczorem zacznie się przymrozek. (vyeh-cho-rem za-ch-nyeh sye pshym-ro-zhek) - Frost will set in the evening.

41. Czasami występują burze piaskowe. (cha-za-mi vis-tsoo-oo boor-zeh pee-ahs-koh-veh) - Sometimes there are sandstorms.

42. W górach są opady śniegu. (v goo-rah sah o-pah-dih shnye-goo) - There is snowfall in the mountains.

43. Wieczorami robi się chłodniej. (vye-cho-ra-mee ro-bee sye cho-lo-dnyey)

Image by <a href="https://www.freepik.com/free-photo/3d-cartoon-background-children_37740730.htm#query=candy%20country&position=17&from_view=search&track=ais">Freepik</a>

Image by <a href="https://www.freepik.com/free-photo/cartoon-style-candy-gummy-bears_40339057.htm#page=2&query=candy%20car&position=2&from_view=search&track=ais">Freepik</a>

Image by <a href="https://www.freepik.com/free-photo/3d-cartoon-background-children_37740744.htm#query=candy%20slide&position=0&from_view=search&track=ais">Freepik</a>

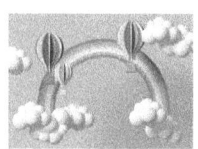

Image by <a href="https://www.freepik.com/free-photo/3d-clouds-hot-air-balloons_14140127.htm#query=Rainbow&position=31&from_view=search&track=sph">Freepik</a>

RUSSIAN

1. She visits her father.

Она навещает своего отца.

Ona poseshchayet ah-tsah

2. I telephone my friend.   Я звоню своему другу.

Ya zvonyou droo-goo.

3. I travel a lot.

Я много путешествую.

Ya mnoga puteshetvuyou.

4. I have a melon.   У меня есть дыня.

Oo menya yest dynya.

Image by <a href="https://www.freepik.com/free-vector/colorful-candy-land-background-hand-drawn-style_2303811.htm#query=Candy%20land&position=11&from_view=search&track=sph">Freepik</a>

5. You take two oranges.

Вы берете два апельсина.

Vy beryote dvah ahpelseenah.

6. I don't like beans.　　Я не люблю бобы.

Mne nye nravitsya fah-sol.

7. I don't like onions.　　Я не люблю лук.

Ya nye lyoublue luke.

8. I drink　　　　　я пью　　yah pyou

9. I drink juice.　　　Я пью сок.　Ya pyou sok.

10. You drink.　　　　Ты пьешь.　Ty pyosh.

11. You drink water.　　Ты пьешь воду.

Ty pyosh Vah-doo.

12. They drink　Они пьют　Ah-nee pyout.

13. They drink water and juice.

Они пьют воду и сок. Ah-nee pyout vah-doo ee sok.

<a href="https://www.freepik.com/free-vector/kawaii-fast-food-cute-donut-coffee-illustration_5769149.htm#query=donut&position=36&from_view=search&track=sph">Image by gstudioimagen</a> on Freepik

14. You make tea.   Ты делаешь чай.

Ty dyelah-yesh chay.

15. I drink water with ice.   Я пью воду со льдом.

Ya pyou vah-doo sahl-dome.

16. She would like milk.   Она хотела бы молока.

Ah-nah hah-tyelah by mah-lah-ko.

17. I am eating eating a sandwich.

я ем бутерброд.   Yah yem booter-brot

18. I am eating a sandwich with cheese.

Я ем бутерброд с сыром. Yah yem booter-brot s syrom.

19. He brings a gift.   Он приносит подарок.

20. He visits his parents every Sunday.

Он навещает своих родителей каждое воскресенье.

21. Do you visit your friends often?

Вы часто навещаете своих друзей?

22. I like tomatoes.   я люблю помидоры.

Mne nrahvyatsa pomidory.

23. He would like black coffee.

Он хотел бы черный кофе.

On ho-tyel koffee.

24. I take a piece of bread.   Я беру кусок хлеба.
Yah beroo koo-sok hleba.

25. We take two pieces of cheese.
Мы Берем два кусочка сыра.
My beryom dva koos-kah syra.

26. Do you have fish?   У вас есть рыба?
Oo vahs yest ree-bah?

27. Where is the salt?   Где соль? Gdye sol?

28. Can you bring me a fork?
Можешь принести мне вилку?
Mozhete preenestee mne veel-koo?

29. Can you bring me a spoon?
Можешь принести мне ложку?
Mozhete preenestee mnye lozh-koo?

30. Do you have a city map?   У вас есть карта города?
OO vahs yest karta go-rahd-ah?

32. Where is the post office?   Где почта?   Gdye poch-tah?

33. Where is the mall?   Где магазин?   Gdye mah-gah-zeen?

34. Where is the pharmacy?   Где находится аптека?
Gdye nah-hoteetsya ahp-tye-kah?

35. We need rice and bread.   Нам нужен рис и хлеб. Nahm noozhin rees ee hah-lyep

36. We need tomatoes for soup. Nahm noozhnee dlyah soop-pah.

37. Where is the grocery store?   Где супермаркет? Gdye toot sooper-mahrket?

38. Where is the market?   Где рынок?   Gdye ree-nok?

39. Do you sell fruits and vegetables?   Вы продаете фрукты и овощи?

Vy prah-dah-yote frook-tee ee o-vahshchee.

40. We sell fruits and vegetables.   Мы продаем фрукты и овощи. My prah-dah-yom frook-tee ee o-vah-shee.

41. I have to buy a book.   Я должен купить книгу.   Mnye noozhnah koopeet kneegoo.

42. I have to go to the bookstore.   я должен пойти в книжный магазин.

Ya dolzhin pie-tee v kneezhnee mah-gah-zeen.

43. I have to go to the super market. Я должен пойти в супермаркет.

Ya dlozhin pie-tee v sooper-market.

USEFUL RUSSIAN PHRASES

2. Спасибо! (Spasibo!) - Thank you!

3. Извините! (Izvinite!) - Excuse me!

4. Да (Da) - Yes

5. Нет (Net) - No

6. Пожалуйста (Pozhaluysta) - Please

7. Как дела? (Kak dela?) - How are you?

8. Я не понимаю. (Ya ne ponimayu.) - I don't understand.

9. Где находится...? (Gde nakhoditsya...?) - Where is...?

10. Сколько это стоит? (Skol'ko eto stoit?) - How much does this cost?

11. Я говорю по-английски. (Ya govoryu po-angliyski.) - I speak English.

12. Приятно познакомиться! (Priyatno poznakomitsya!) - Nice to meet you!

13. Меня зовут... (Menya zovut...) - My name is...

14. Я вас не понимаю. (Ya vas ne ponimayu.) - I don't understand you.

15. Помогите, пожалуйста. (Pomogite, pozhaluysta.) - Help me, please.

16. Как вас зовут? (Kak vas zovut?) - What is your name?

17. Я из... (Ya iz...) - I am from...

18. Добрый день! (Dobryy den'!) - Good day!

19. Извините! (Izvinite!) - I'm sorry!

20. До свидания! (Do svidaniya!) - Goodbye!

21. Я благодарю вас! (Ya blagodaryu vas!) - I thank you!

22. Я не знаю. (Ya ne znayu.) - I don't know.

23. Что делать? (Chto delat'?) - What to do?

24. Вы говорите по-английски? (Vy govorite po-angliyski?) - Do you speak English?

25. Как я могу помочь? (Kak ya mogu pomoch'?) - How can I help?

26. Где находится туалет? (Gde nakhoditsya tualet?) - Where is the restroom?

27. У меня голод. (U menya golod.) - I am hungry.

28. Мне хочется пить. (Mne khochetsya pit') - I want to drink.

29. Я устал/устала. (Ya ustal/ustala.) - I am tired.

30. Я счастлив/счастлива. (Ya schastliv/schastliva.) - I am happy.

31. Спасибо за все. (Spasibo za vse.) - Thank you for everything.

32. Я вас люблю. (Ya vas lyublyu.) - I love you.

33. Доброе утро! (Dobroe utro!) - Good morning!

34. Добрый вечер! (Dobryy vecher!) - Good evening!

35. Я слушаю музыку. (Ya slushayu muzyku.) - I am listening to music.

36. Я смотрю телевизор. (Ya smotryu televizor.) - I am watching TV.

37. Я читаю книгу. (Ya chitayu knigu.) - I am reading a book.

38. Я иду домой. (Ya idu domoy.) - I am going home.

39. Где вы живете? (Gde vy zhivete?) - Where do you live?

40. Я занят/занята. (Ya zanyat/zanyata.) - I am busy.

41. Я учусь в университете. (Ya uchusʹ v universitete.) - I study at the university.

42. Я хочу отдохнуть. (Ya khochu otdokhnutʹ) - I want to relax.

43. Я хочу встретиться с коллегами. (Ya khochu vstretitʹsya s kollegami.) - I want to meet with colleagues.

44. Добро пожаловать! (Dobro pozhalovatʹ!) - Welcome!

45. Я проголодался/проголодалась. (Ya progolodal/progolodala.) - I am hungry.

46. Я потерялся/потерялась. (Ya poteryalsya/poteryalasʹ) - I am lost.

47. Можно вас попросить? (Mozhno vas poprositʹ?) - Can I ask you for a favor?

48. Казино, пожалуйста. (Kazino, pozhaluysta.) - Casino, please.

49. Мне нужна помощь. (Mne nuzhna pomoshchʹ) - I need help.

50. Я хочу заказать еду. (Ya khochu zakazatʹ edu.) - I want to order food.

51. Где я могу найти такси? (Gde ya mogu nayti taksi?) - Where can I find a taxi?

52. Я хочу арендовать автомобиль. (Ya khochu arendovatʹ avtomobilʹ) - I want to rent a car.

53. Расположение гостиницы, пожалуйста. (Raspolozhenie gostinitsy, pozhaluysta.) - Hotel location, please.

54. Как добраться до аэропорта? (Kak dobratʹsya do aeroporta?) - How to get to the airport?

55. Это место закрыто? (Eto mesto zakryto?) - Is this place closed?

56. Я хочу купить сувениры. (Ya khochu kupitʹ suveniry.) - I want to buy souvenirs.

57. Где я могу снять фотографию? (Gde ya mogu snyat' fotografiiu?) - Where can I take a photo?

58. Водитель, пожалуйста. (Voditel', pozhaluysta.) - Driver, please.

59. Где я могу получить помощь? (Gde ya mogu poluchit' pomoshch'?) - Where can I get assistance?

60. Я не могу найти свой отель. (Ya ne mogu nayti svoi otel') - I can't find my hotel.

61. Я ищу ресторан с местной кухней. (Ya ishchu restoran s mestnoy kuhney.) - I am looking for a restaurant with local cuisine.

62. Можно попросить счет, пожалуйста? (Mozhno poprosit' schet, pozhaluysta?) - Can I have the bill, please?

63. Где находится ближайшая аптека? (Gde nakhoditsya blizhayshaya apteka?) - Where is the nearest pharmacy?

64. Что обязательно стоит посетить здесь? (Chto obyazatel'no stoit posetit' zdes'?) - What are the must-visit places here?

65. Я хочу забронировать номер. (Ya khochu zabronirovat' nomer.) - I want to book a room.

66. Куда можно пойти вечером? (Kuda mozhno poyti vecherom?) - Where can I go in the evening?

67. Я ищу местное кафе. (Ya ishchu mestnoe kafe.) - I am looking for a local cafe.

68. Где я могу снять велосипед? (Gde ya mogu snyat' velosiped?) - Where can I rent a bicycle?

69. Можно попросить помощи у переводчика? (Mozhno poprosit' pomoschi u perevodchika?) - Can I ask for help from a translator?

70. Я потерял/потеряла свою кредитную карту. (Ya poteryal/poteryala svoyu kreditnuyu kartu.) - I lost my credit card.

71. Можно вас фотографировать? (Mozhno vas fotografirovat'?) - Can I take your photo?

72. Я хочу отправить эту открытку. (Ya khochu otpravit' etu otkrytku.) - I want to send this postcard.

73. Возможно ли безналичное расчёт? (Vozmozhno li beznalichnoe raschot?) - Is cashless payment possible?

74. Я потерял/потеряла свои документы. (Ya poteryal/poteryala svoi dokumenty.) - I lost my documents.

75. Где я могу снять номер в гостинице? (Gde ya mogu snyat' nomer v gostinitse?) - Where can I get a hotel room?

76. Я хочу сделать экскурсию. (Ya khochu sdelat' ekskursiyu.) - I want to take a tour.

77. Где я могу отправить почтовую открытку? (Gde ya mogu otpravit' pochtovuyu otkrytku?) - Where can I send a postcard?

78. Я потерял/потеряла свой багаж. (Ya poteryal/poteryala svoi bagazh.) - I lost my luggage.

79. Можно попросить помощи у полиции? (Mozhno poprosit' pomoschi u politsii?) - Can I ask for help from the police?

80. Я хочу посмотреть местные достопримечательности. (Ya khochu posmotret' mestnye dostoprimechatelnosti.) - I want to see local attractions.

81. Где я могу снять машину? (Gde ya mogu snyat' mashinu?) - Where can I rent a car?

82. Можно пойти пешком до центра? (Mozhno poiti peshkom do tsentra?) - Can I walk to the city center?

83. Я потерял/потеряла свой телефон. (Ya poteryal/poteryala svoi telefon.) - I lost my phone.

84. Какой автобус идет в аэропорт? (Kakoy avtobus idet v aeroport?) - Which bus goes to the airport?

a href="https://www.freepik.com/free-photo/towering-skyscraper-with-bulbous-generative-ai_40333709.htm#query=candy%20castle&position=1&from_view=search&track=ais">Image by masadepan</a> on Freepik

RUSSIAN AIRPORT PHRASES

1. Здравствуйте! (Zdravstvuyte!) - Hello!

2. Спасибо! (Spasibo!) - Thank you!

3. Извините! (Izvinite!) - Excuse me!

4. Да (Da) - Yes

5. Нет (Net) - No

6. Пожалуйста (Pozhaluysta) - Please

7. Как дела? (Kak dela?) - How are you?

8. Я не понимаю. (Ya ne ponimayu.) - I don't understand.

9. Где находится...? (Gde nakhoditsya...?) - Where is...?

10. Сколько это стоит? (Skol'ko eto stoit?) - How much does this cost?

11. Я говорю по-английски. (Ya govoryu po-angliyski.) - I speak English.

12. Приятно познакомиться! (Priyatno poznakomitsya!) - Nice to meet you!

13. Меня зовут... (Menya zovut...) - My name is...

14. Я вас не понимаю. (Ya vas ne ponimayu.) - I don't understand you.

15. Помогите, пожалуйста. (Pomogite, pozhaluysta.) - Help me, please.

16. Как вас зовут? (Kak vas zovut?) - What is your name?

17. Я из... (Ya iz...) - I am from...

18. Добрый день! (Dobryy den') - Good day!

19. Извините! (Izvinite!) - I'm sorry!

20. До свидания! (Do svidaniya!) - Goodbye!

21. Я благодарю вас! (Ya blagodaryu vas!) - I thank you!

22. Я не знаю. (Ya ne znayu.) - I don't know.

23. Что делать? (Chto delat'?) - What to do?

24. Вы говорите по-английски? (Vy govorite po-angliyski?) - Do you speak English?

25. Как я могу помочь? (Kak ya mogu pomoch'?) - How can I help?

26. Где находится туалет? (Gde nakhoditsya tualet?) - Where is the restroom?

27. У меня голод. (U menya golod.) - I am hungry.

28. Мне хочется пить. (Mne khochetsya pit') - I want to drink.

29. Я устал/устала. (Ya ustal/ustala.) - I am tired.

30. Я счастлив/счастлива. (Ya schastliv/schastliva.) - I am happy.

31. Спасибо за все. (Spasibo za vse.) - Thank you for everything.

32. Я вас люблю. (Ya vas lyublyu.) - I love you.

33. Доброе утро! (Dobroe utro!) - Good morning!

34. Добрый вечер! (Dobryy vecher!) - Good evening!

35. Я слушаю музыку. (Ya slushayu muzyku.) - I am listening to music.

36. Я смотрю телевизор. (Ya smotryu televizor.) - I am watching TV.

37. Я читаю книгу. (Ya chitayu knigu.) - I am reading a book.

38. Я иду домой. (Ya idu domoy.) - I am going home.

39. Где вы живете? (Gde vy zhivete?) - Where do you live?

40. Я занят/занята. (Ya zanyat/zanyata.) - I am busy.

41. Я учусь в университете. (Ya uchus' v universitete.) - I study at the university.

42. Я хочу отдохнуть. (Ya khochu otdokhnut') - I want to relax.

43. Я хочу встретиться с коллегами. (Ya khochu vstretit'sya s kollegami.) - I want to meet with colleagues.

44. Добро пожаловать! (Dobro pozhalovat'!) - Welcome!

45. Я проголодался/проголодалась. (Ya progolodal/progolodala.) - I am hungry.

46. Я потерялся/потерялась. (Ya poteryalsya/poteryalas') - I am lost.

47. Можно вас попросить? (Mozhno vas poprosit'?) - Can I ask you for a favor?

48. Казино, пожалуйста. (Kazino, pozhaluysta.) - Casino, please.

49. Мне нужна помощь. (Mne nuzhna pomoshch') - I need help.

50. Я хочу заказать еду. (Ya khochu zakazat' edu.) - I want to order food.

51. Где я могу найти такси? (Gde ya mogu nayti taksi?) - Where can I find a taxi?

52. Я хочу арендовать автомобиль. (Ya khochu arendovat' avtomobil') - I want to rent a car.

53. Расположение гостиницы, пожалуйста. (Raspolozhenie gostinitsy, pozhaluysta.) - Hotel location, please.

54. Как добраться до аэропорта? (Kak dobrat'sya do aeroporta?) - How to get to the airport?

55. Это место закрыто? (Eto mesto zakryto?) - Is this place closed?

56. Я хочу купить сувениры. (Ya khochu kupit' suveniry.) - I want to buy souvenirs.

57. Где я могу снять фотографию? (Gde ya mogu snyat' fotografiiu?) - Where can I take a photo?

58. Водитель, пожалуйста. (Voditel', pozhaluysta.) - Driver, please.

59. Где я могу получить помощь? (Gde ya mogu poluchit' pomoshch'?) - Where can I get assistance?

60. Я не могу найти свой отель. (Ya ne mogu nayti svoi otel') - I can't find my hotel.

61. Я ищу ресторан с местной кухней. (Ya ishchu restoran s mestnoy kuhney.) - I am looking for a restaurant with local cuisine.

62. Можно попросить счет, пожалуйста? (Mozhno poprosit' schet, pozhaluysta?) - Can I have the bill, please?

63. Где находится ближайшая аптека? (Gde nakhoditsya blizhayshaya apteka?) - Where is the nearest pharmacy?

64. Что обязательно стоит посетить здесь? (Chto obyazatel'no stoit posetit' zdes'?) - What are the must-visit places here?

65. Я хочу забронировать номер. (Ya khochu zabronirovat' nomer.) - I want to book a room.

66. Куда можно пойти вечером? (Kuda mozhno poyti vecherom?) - Where can I go in the evening?

67. Я ищу местное кафе. (Ya ishchu mestnoe kafe.) - I am looking for a local cafe.

68. Где я могу снять велосипед? (Gde ya mogu snyat' velosiped?) - Where can I rent a bicycle?

69. Можно попросить помощи у переводчика? (Mozhno poprosit' pomoschi u perevodchika?) - Can I ask for help from a translator?

70. Я потерял/потеряла свою кредитную карту. (Ya poteryal/poteryala svoyu kreditnuyu kartu.) - I lost my credit card.

71. Можно вас фотографировать? (Mozhno vas fotografirovat'?) - Can I take your photo?

72. Я хочу отправить эту открытку. (Ya khochu otpravit' etu otkrytku.) - I want to send this postcard.

73. Возможно ли безналичное расчёт? (Vozmozhno li beznalichnoe raschot?) - Is cashless payment possible?

74. Я потерял/потеряла свои документы. (Ya poteryal/poteryala svoi dokumenty.) - I lost my documents.

75. Где я могу снять номер в гостинице? (Gde ya mogu snyat' nomer v gostinitse?) - Where can I get a hotel room?

76. Я хочу сделать экскурсию. (Ya khochu sdelat' ekskursiyu.) - I want to take a tour.

77. Где я могу отправить почтовую открытку? (Gde ya mogu otpravit' pochtovuyu otkrytku?) - Where can I send a postcard?

78. Я потерял/потеряла свой багаж. (Ya poteryal/poteryala svoi bagazh.) - I lost my luggage.

79. Можно попросить помощи у полиции? (Mozhno poprosit' pomoschi u politsii?) - Can I ask for help from the police?

80. Я хочу посмотреть местные достопримечательности. (Ya khochu posmotret' mestnye dostoprimechatelnosti.) - I want to see local attractions.

81. Где я могу снять машину? (Gde ya mogu snyat' mashinu?) - Where can I rent a car?

82. Можно пойти пешком до центра? (Mozhno poiti peshkom do tsentra?) - Can I walk to the city center?

83. Я потерял/потеряла свой телефон. (Ya poteryal/poteryala svoi telefon.) - I lost my phone.

84. Какой автобус идет в аэропорт? (Kakoy avtobus idet v aeroport?) - Which bus goes to the airport?

< a href="https://www.freepik.com/free-photo/towering-skyscraper-with-bulbous-generative-ai_40333709.htm#query=candy%20castle&position=1&from_view=search&track=ais">Image by masadepan</a> on Freepik

RUSSIAN BUSINESS PHRASES

1. Работа (Rabota) - Job
2. Резюме (Rezyume) - Resume/CV
3. Вакансия (Vakansiya) - Vacancy
4. Карьера (Kar'era) - Career
5. Занятость (Zanyatost') - Employment
6. Собеседование (Sobesedovaniye) - Interview
7. Работодатель (Rabotodatel') - Employer
8. Сотрудник (Sotrudnik) - Employee
9. Трудоустройство (Trudoustroystvo) - Employment/Job placement
10. Отпуск (Otpusk) - Vacation/Leave
11. Зарплата (Zarplata) - Salary/Wage
12. Сверка (Sverka) - Job offer
13. Увольнение (Uvol'neniye) - Termination/Dismissal
14. Профессия (Professiya) - Profession/Occupation
15. Открытая позиция (Otkrytaya pozitsiya) - Open position/Vacancy
16. Трудовой договор (Trudovoy dogovor) - Employment contract
17. Найм (Naym) - Hiring
18. Подписать контракт (Podpisat' kontrakt) - Sign a contract

19. Квалификации (Kvalifikatsii) - Qualifications

20. Повышение зарплаты (Povysheniye zarplaty) - Salary raise

21. График работы (Grafik raboty) - Work schedule

22. Курсы повышения квалификации (Kursy povysheniya kvalifikatsii) - Professional development courses

23. Отдел кадров (Otdel kadrov) - Human Resources department

24. Рабочее место (Rabocheye mesto) - Workplace

25. Развитие карьеры (Razvitiye kar'ery) - Career development

26. Переговоры о зарплате (Peregovory o zarplate) - Salary negotiations

27. Трудоустроиться (Trudoustroit'sya) - Get employed

28. Командир (Komandir) - Supervisor/Manager

29. Должностные обязанности (Dolzhnostnyye obyazannosti) - Job duties

30. Уровень зарплаты (Uroven' zarplaty) - Salary level

31. Повышение квалификации (Povysheniye kvalifikatsii) - Skills enhancement

32. Отработанные часы (Otrabotannyye chasy) - Worked hours

33. Рынок труда (Rynok truda) - Labor market

34. Претендовать на должность (Pretendovat' na dolzhnost') - Apply for a position

35. Опыт работы (Opyt raboty) - Work experience

36. Рекомендации (Rekomendatsii) - Recommendations

37. Престижная работа (Prestizhnaya rabota) - Prestigious job

38. Перерыв на обед (Pereryv na obed) - Lunch break

39. Профессиональные навыки (Professional'nyye navyki) - Professional skills

40. Временная работа (Vremennoye rabota) - Temporary job

41. Сокращение штатов (Sokrashcheniye shtatov) - Downsizing/Layoffs

42. Командировка (Komandirovka) - Business trip

43. Вознаграждение (Voznagrazhdeniye) - Remuneration/Compensation

44. Вступительное испытание (Vstupitel'noye ispytaniye) - Entrance examination

45. Сотрудничество (Sotrudnichestvo) - Collaboration/Cooperation

46. Сокращение рабочего времени (Sokrashcheniye rabochego vremeni) - Reduction of working hours

47. Оплата труда (Oplata truda) - Payment for work

48. Возможности для карьерного роста (Vozmozhnosti dlya kar'ernogo rosta) - Opportunities for career growth

49. Поддержка сотрудников (Podderzhka sotrudnikov) - Employee support

50. Перспективы развития (Perspektivy razvitiya) - Development prospects

Numbers 1-100 in Russian

1 - один (a-DIN)

2 - два (dva)

3 - три (tree)

4 - четыре (chee-TY-re)

5 - пять (pyat')

6 - шесть (shest')

7 - семь (syem')

8 - восемь (vo-syem')

9 - девять (dyev-YAT')

10 - десять (dyes-YAT')

11 - одиннадцать (a-deen-NAH-tset')

12 - двенадцать (dvee-NAH-tsat')

13 - тринадцать (tree-NAH-tsat')

14 - четырнадцать (chee-tyr-NAH-tsat')

15 - пятнадцать (pyat-NAH-tsat')

16 - шестнадцать (shest-NAH-tsat')

17 - семнадцать (syem-NAH-tsat')

18 - восемнадцать (vo-syem-NAH-tsat')

19 - девятнадцать (dyev-YAT-naht-syat')

20 - двадцать (dva-DZAT')

21 - двадцать один (dva-DZAT' a-DIN)

22 - двадцать два (dva-DZAT' dva)

23 - двадцать три (dva-DZAT' tree)

24 - двадцать четыре (dva-DZAT' chee-TY-re)

25 - двадцать пять (dva-DZAT' pyat')

26 - двадцать шесть (dva-DZAT' shest')

27 - двадцать семь (dva-DZAT' syem')

28 - двадцать восемь (dva-DZAT' vo-syem')

29 - двадцать девять (dva-DZAT' dyev-YAT')

30 - тридцать (tree-DZAT')

31 - тридцать один (tree-DZAT' a-DIN)

32 - тридцать два (tree-DZAT' dva)

33 - тридцать три (tree-DZAT' tree)

34 - тридцать четыре (tree-DZAT' chee-TY-re)

35 - тридцать пять (tree-DZAT' pyat')

36 - тридцать шесть (tree-DZAT' shest')

37 - тридцать семь (tree-DZAT' syem')

38 - тридцать восемь (tree-DZAT' vo-syem')

39 - тридцать девять (tree-DZAT' dyev-YAT')

40 - сорок (SOR-ak)

41 - сорок один (SOR-ak a-DIN)

42 - сорок два (SOR-ak dva)

43 - сорок три (SOR-ak tree)

44 - сорок четыре (SOR-ak chee-TY-re)

45 - сорок пять (SOR-ak pyat')

46 - сорок шесть (SOR-ak shest')

47 - сорок семь (SOR-ak syem')

48 - сорок восемь (SOR-ak vo-syem')

49 - сорок девять (SOR-ak dyev-YAT')

50 - пятьдесят (pyat'-DYEs-yat')

51 - пятьдесят один (pyat'-DYEs-yat' a-DIN)

52 - пятьдесят два (pyat'-DYEs-yat' dva)

53 - пятьдесят три (pyat'-DYEs-yat' tree)

54 - пятьдесят четыре (pyat'-DYEs-yat' chee-TY-re)

55 - пятьдесят пять (pyat'-DYEs-yat' pyat')

56 - пятьдесят шесть (pyat'-DYEs-yat' shest')

57 - пятьдесят семь (pyat'-DYEs-yat' syem')

58 - пятьдесят восемь (pyat'-DYEs-yat' vo-syem')

59 - пятьдесят девять (pyat'-DYEs-yat' dyev-YAT')

60 - шестьдесят (shest'-DYEs-yat')

61 - шестьдесят один (shest'-DYEs-yat' a-DIN)

62 - шестьдесят два (shest'-DYEs-yat' dva)

63 - шестьдесят три (shest'-DYEs-yat' tree)

64 - шестьдесят четыре (shest'-DYEs-yat' chee-TY-re)

65 - шестьдесят пять (shest'-DYEs-yat' pyat')

66 - шестьдесят шесть (shest'-DYEs-yat' shest')

67 - шестьдесят семь (shest'-DYEs-yat' syem')

68 - шестьдесят восемь (shest'-DYEs-yat' vo-syem')

69 - шестьдесят девять (shest'-DYEs-yat' dyev-YAT')

70 - семьдесят (syem'-DYEs-yat')

71 - семьдесят один (syem'-DYEs-yat' a-DIN)

72 - семьдесят два (syem'-DYEs-yat' dva)

73 - семьдесят три (syem'-DYEs-yat' tree)

74 - семьдесят четыре (syem'-DYEs-yat' chee-TY-re)

75 - семьдесят пять (syem'-DYEs-yat' pyat')

76 - семьдесят шесть (syem'-DYEs-yat' shest')

77 - семьдесят семь (syem'-DYEs-yat' syem')

78 - семьдесят восемь (syem'-DYEs-yat' vo-syem')

79 - семьдесят девять (syem'-DYEs-yat' dyev-YAT')

80 - восемьдесят (vo-syem'-DYEs-yat')

81 - восемьдесят один (vo-syem'-DYEs-yat' a-DIN)

82 - восемьдесят два (vo-syem'-DYEs-yat' dva)
83 - восемьдесят три (vo-syem'-DYEs-yat' tree)
84 - восемьдесят четыре (vo-syem'-DYEs-yat' chee-TY-re)
85 - восемьдесят пять (vo-syem'-DYEs-yat' pyat')
86 - восемьдесят шесть (vo-syem'-DYEs-yat' shest')
87 - восемьдесят семь (vo-syem'-DYEs-yat' syem')
88 - восемьдесят восемь (vo-syem'-DYEs-yat' vo-syem')
89 - восемьдесят девять (vo-syem'-DYEs-yat' dyev-YAT')
90 - девяносто (dyev-ya-NO-sto)
91 - девяносто один (dyev-ya-NO-sto a-DIN)
92 - девяносто два (dyev-ya-NO-sto dva)
93 - девяносто три (dyev-ya-NO-sto tree)
94 - девяносто четыре (dyev-ya-NO-sto chee-TY-re)
95 - девяносто пять (dyev-ya-NO-sto pyat')
96 - девяносто шесть (dyev-ya-NO-sto shest')
97 - девяносто семь (dyev-ya-NO-sto syem')
98 - девяносто восемь (dyev-ya-NO-sto vo-syem')
99 - девяносто девять (dyev-ya-NO-sto dyev-YAT')
100 - сто (sto)

USEFUL POST OFFICE PHRASES IN RUSSIAN

1. Здравствуйте (ZDRAST-vooy-tye) - Hello

2. Я хотел бы отправить письмо (YA kho-TYEL by ot-PRAY-veet' PIS'-mo) - I would like to send a letter.

3. Сколько стоит отправить посылку за границу? (SKOL-ka STO-eet ot-PRAY-teet' pah-SYL-koo za gra-DITS-oo) - How much does it cost to send a package overseas?

4. Я хотел бы купить марки (YA kho-TYEL by KOO-pit' MAR-kee) - I would like to buy stamps.

5. Где находится почтовое отделение? (gdy na-kha-DEETS-ya pa-CHTO-va-ye a-dye-LEN-ye) - Where is the post office located?

6. Могу я отправить этот пакет здесь? (MA-goo ya ot-PRAY-teet' EHTOT pa-KYET zdyes') - Can I send this package from here?

7. Я потерял/а почтовый адрес (YA pa-tye-RAL/a pa-CHTOW-yee a-DREES) - I've lost my mailing address.

8. Я хотел бы получить почтовый ящик (YA kho-TYEL by pa-LU-cheet' pa-CHTOW-yee YASH-ik) - I would like to get a mailbox.

9. Как долго занимает доставка письма в другую страну? (kak DOL-ga za-nee-MA-yet da-stav-ka PEES-ma v DROO-goo stro-NOO) - How long does it take for a letter to be delivered to another country?

10. Когда будет доставлено мое письмо? (KOG-da BYET dost-av-LE-na MOH-yeh PEES-ma) - When will my letter be delivered?

11. У меня есть письмо для вас (OO MYE-nye-yest PEES-ma dlya vas) - I have a letter for you.

12. Я хотел бы отправить эту открытку внутрь страны (YA kho-TYEL by ot-PRAY-teet' EHTOO AT-kryt-koo VNOOTR stro-NY) - I would like to send this postcard within the country.

13. Мне нужен регистрированный почтовый отправления (MNYE NOO-zhen ree-gis-tee-ro-VAN-ny pa-CHTO-vy otp-RAV-lyen-ee-ye) - I need a registered mail shipment.

14. Я хотел бы изменить получателя (YA kho-TYEL by ee-ZME-neet' pa-loo-CHA-tye-la) - I would like to change the recipient.

15. Сколько времени занимает доставка почты внутри страны? (SKOL-ka vre-MYE-nee za-nee-MA-yet DA-stav-ka PACH-tee VNOO-tree STRO-nee) - How long does it take for mail to be delivered within the country?

16. Мне нужно заполнить форму доставки (MNYE NOO-zhna zap-nee-LEET' FOR-moo DA-stav-kee) - I need to fill out a delivery form.

17. Я не получил уведомление о посылке (YA nye po-lo-ZHEEL BOO-vye-DEE-mye o pa-SYL-kye) - I didn't receive a notification about the package.

18. Могу я отправить документы экспресс почтой? (MA-goo YA ot-PRAY-teet' DO-koo-MEN-ty EHKS-press PA-choy) - Can I send documents by express mail?

19. Будет ли доставка завтра? (BOO-dyet lee DA-stav-ka zaf-TRA) - Will there be delivery tomorrow?

20. Я хотел бы отследить мой пакет (YA kho-TYEL by ot-SLYE-dit' MOY pa-KYET)

21. Какая максимальная весовая нагрузка для отправки? (ka-KA-ya mak-si-MAHL'-naya vye-SO-va-ya na-GROOS-ka dlya at-PRAY-kee) - What is the maximum weight limit for shipping?

22. У меня потерян чек за почтовую отправку (OO MYE-nya pa-tye-RAN chek za pa-CHTOW-yu at-PRAD-ku) - I've lost the receipt for the mail shipment.

23. Вы можете сделать копию этого документа? (VY ma-GYE-tye SYE-la-t' KA-pee-YOO EH-ta-va do-ku-MEN-ta) - Can you make a copy of this document?

24. Могу я получить опись пересылки? (MA-goo ya pa-LOO-cheet' a-PEES' pye-ree-SIL-kee) - Can I get a receipt for the shipment?

25. Куда мне обратиться для уточнения статуса почтовой отправки? (KOO-da mnye ab-RA-TEET'-sya dlya oo-TOCH-ni-ya STA-too-sa pa-CHTOW-yee at-PRAD-kee) - Where can I inquire about the status of my mail shipment?

26. Я не могу найти мой трекинг-номер (YA nye ma-GOO na-EET' MOYN TRE-keeng NO-myer) - I can't find my tracking number.

27. Какой размер коробки мне нужно получить для отправки? (KA-koy raz-MYER ka-ROB-kee mnye NOOZH-na pa-LOO-cheet' dlya at-PRAD-kee) - What size box do I need to get for shipping?

28. Я хотел бы отправить ценный груз (YA kho-TYEL by at-PRAY-teet' TSYEN-ny groos) - I would like to send valuable cargo.

29. Отправить эти документы по почте (at-PRAY-teet' EHT-ee do-ku-MEN-ty pa PACH-tye) - Send these documents by mail.

30. Какой адрес надо написать на конверте? (ka-KOY a-DRES na-DA na-PEE-sat' na kan-VYER-tye) - What address should I write on the envelope?

31. Мне нужна помощь с упаковкой товаров (MNYE NOOZHN-a pa-MOSCH' s oo-PAH-kav-koy to-VA-rov) - I need help with packing goods.

32. Почта работает в выходные дни? (PACH-ta ra-BA-ta-yet v vy-KHOOD-nye dnee) - Does the post office work on weekends?

33. Это находится далеко отсюда? (EH-ta na-kha-DEET-sya da-LEE-ka at-SYOO-da) - Is it far from here?

34. Я хотел бы отследить мою посылку (YA kho-TYEL by ot-SLYE-dit' MOO-yu pa-SYL-ku) - I would like to track my package.

USEFUL WEATHER PHRASES IN RUSSIAN

1. Погода хорошая (PA-go-da ho-RO-sha-ya) - The weather is good.

2. Сегодня солнечно (SYE-vo-dnya sal-NECH-na) - Today is sunny.

3. Завтра будет дождь (ZAV-tra BUD-yet DOZHD') - Tomorrow will be rainy.

4. Вчера был снегопад (VCHYE-ra byl SNE-go-pad) - Yesterday there was a snowfall.

5. Сейчас туман (SYE-chas TOO-man) - It is foggy right now.

6. Возьмите зонт, будет гроза (VAZ'-mi-tye ZONT, BUD-yet GRO-za) - Take an umbrella, there will be a storm.

7. Сегодня очень жарко (SYE-vo-dnya o-CHEN' ZHAHR-ka) - It is very hot today.

8. Ветер дует сильно (VYE-tyer DOO-yet SEEL'-na) - The wind is blowing strongly.

9. На улице холодно (na ool-TEE-tse kha-LOD-na) - It is cold outside.

10. Будет тепло завтра (BOO-dyet TE-plo ZAV-tra) - It will be warm tomorrow.

11. Небо чистое (NEE-bo CHEES-to-ye) - The sky is clear.

12. Воздух свежий (voz-DOOCH SVYE-zhii) - The air is fresh.

13. Погода переменчивая (pa-GO-da pee-ryen-MCHEE-va-ya) - The weather is changeable.

14. Осадки ожидаются (o-SAHD-kee o-zhi-DA-yut-sya) - Precipitation is expected.

15. Температура поднимается (tyem-pe-ra-TOO-ra pad-NEE-ma-yes-ya) - The temperature is rising.

16. Скоро будет снег (SKO-ro BOO-dyet snek) - It will snow soon.

17. Давление высокое (da-VLE-nee ve-SA-ko-ye) - The pressure is high.

18. Сегодня влажно (syeh-VO-dnya vla-ZH-no) - It is humid today.

19. В южном направлении ветер (v yuZH-nom na-prav-LEE-nee-ee VYE-ter) - The wind is coming from the south.

20. Пасмурная погода (pas-MOOR-na-ya pa-GO-da) - It is cloudy weather.

21. Прогноз погоды (pro-GNOZ pa-GO-da) - Weather forecast.

22. Утром будет туман (OO-trom BOO-dyet too-MAN) - There will be fog in the morning.

23. Вечером ожидается гроза (vee-CHE-ro-m o-zhi-DA-yet-sya GRO-za) - A storm is expected in the evening.

24. Наступила зима (nas-TOO-pe-la ZEE-ma) - Winter has arrived.

25. Лето наступает (LYE-ta nas-TOO-pa-yet) - Summer is coming.

26. Осенью дождливо (O-SEH-nyu dozh-DEE-vo) - It is rainy in autumn.

27. Весной распускаются цветы (VES-noy ras-PUS-ka-yut-sya tsvye-TEE) - Flowers bloom in spring.

28. В море идут бушующие волны (v MO-rye ee-DOOT boo-SHOO-yusht-ee vol-NY) - There are roaring waves in the sea.

29. Был легкий мороз (byl lyek-KEEY MO-roz) - There was a light frost.

30. Жаркий климат (ZHAHR-keey klee-MAT) - Hot climate.

31. Ощущается ветер (osh-CHOOSH-ya-et-sya VYE-ter) - The wind can be felt.

32. Воздух сырой (voz-DOOCH sy-ROY) - The air is damp.

33. Град (grad) - Hail.

34. Восточный ветер (vas-toch-NEEY VYE-ter) - Eastern wind.

35. Удушающая жара (oo-DOOSH-yash-chay-a ZHA-ra) - Suffocating heat.

36. Буря (BOO-rya) - Storm.

37. Морозно и солнечно (mor-OZ-no ee sal-NECH-no) - Frosty and sunny.

38. Тучи (TOO-chee) - Clouds.

39. Сухой ветер (SOO-khoy VYE-ter) - Dry wind.

40. Влажная погода (vla-ZH-na-ya pa-GO-da) - Humid weather.

41. Сырой климат (SY-roy klee-MAT) - Damp climate.

42. Температура падает (tyem-pe-ra-TOO-ra pa-DYE-yet) - The temperature is dropping.

43. Снег идет (snyek ee-DYOT) - It is snowing.

44. Метель (mye-TYEL') - Blizzard.

45. Вечер будет прохладным (VEE-cher BOO-dyet pra-KHLAD-nym) - The evening will be cool.

46. Пасмурно с прояснениями (pas-MOOR-no s pra-ya-SNYE-nee-ya-mee) - Partly cloudy.

47. Сегодня ветрено (syeh-VO-dnya vyet-RE-na) - It is windy today.

48. Очень холодно (o-CHEN' kha-LOD-na) - It is very cold.

49. Воздух душный (voz-DOOCH DOOSH-nyi) - The air is stuffy.

50. Осенняя листва (o-SYE-nyaya LEES-tva) - Autumn foliage.

USEFUL HOLIDAY PHRASES IN RUSSIAN

1. С наступающим Новым годом! (S na-stu-PA-yu-shchim No-vym go-DOM) - Happy New Year!

2. Весёлого Рождества! (Ves-YO-la-vo Razh-DEStva) - Merry Christmas!

3. С праздником! (S PRAZ-ni-kom) - Happy holidays!

4. Счастливого Рождества! (SCHAST-lee-vo Razh-DEStva) - Happy Christmas!

5. Поздравляю с Новым годом! (Paz-DRAV-lya-yu s No-vym go-DOM) - Congratulations on the New Year!

6. Желаю волшебных праздников! (ZHE-la-yu vol-SHEB-nykh prazd-nee-kov) - Wishing you magical holidays!

7. Удачного Нового года! (U-daCHNO-va No-VO-va go-DA) - Have a successful New Year!

8. Пусть сбудутся все мечты в новом году! (PUST sboo-DOOT-sya vse mech-TY v no-VOM go-DOO) - May all your dreams come true in the new year!

9. Счастья и здоровья в наступающем году! (Schas-TYA i zdo-RO-ve-ya v nas-tu-PA-yu-shchem go-DU) - Happiness and good health in the coming year!

10. Пусть год будет ярким и успешным! (PUST got BU-det YARK-im i oo-SHESTV-nym) - May the year be bright and successful!

11. Зимние каникулы (ZIM-ni-ye ka-nee-KOO-ly) - Winter vacation

12. Рождественский ужин (Razh-DEST-ven-skiy oo-ZHEEN) - Christmas dinner

13. Новогоднее настроение (No-vo-GOD-nye na-stra-NYEn-ye) - New Year mood

14. Семейные праздники (Se-MYE-nye praz-DNEE-ki) - Family celebrations

15. Светящиеся огни (SVYET-yash-chi-ye O-gni) - Shining lights
16. Елочная игрушка (Ye-LOCH-na-ya ig-ROOSH-ka) - Christmas ornament
17. Горячий шоколад (GO-rya-chiy sho-KO-lad) - Hot chocolate
18. Новогодний костюм (No-vo-GOD-ny kahs-TYUM) - New Year costume
19. Загадать желание (za-ga-DAT' zhe-la-NEE-ye) - Make a wish
20. Дарить подарки (DA-reet' po-DAR-ki) - Give presents
21. Праздничный наряд (praz-DNEECH-niy na-RYAD) - Festive attire
22. Зимний пейзаж (ZIM-niy PAI-zazh) - Winter landscape
23. Рождественская звезда (Razh-DES-ten-skaya ZVEZ-da) - Christmas star
24. Сказочные мгновения (SKA-zochnye mGNO-vye-nya) - Magical moments
25. Волшебный снег (vol-SHEB-nyy snek) - Enchanting snow
26. Резьба по дереву (REZ'-ba po DER-ye-voo) - Wood carving
27. Зимний спорт (ZIM-niy sport) - Winter sport
28. Шампанское и треск фейерверков (sham-PANS-ka-ye i TRESK fyeer-ver-kof) - Champagne and fireworks
29. Зимняя сказка (ZIM-nya-ya SKAZ-ka) - Winter fairytale
30. Снеговик и снежный ком (sne-GO-vik i SNEZH-nyy kom) - Snowman and snowball
31. Мороженое и фрукты (ma-ro-ZHE-ne-ye i FROOK-ty) - Ice cream and fruits
32. Свечи и ароматы (SVE-chee i a-ro-MA-ty) - Candles and scents
33. Гирлянды и украшения (gir-LYAN-dy i uk-RA-she-NYA) - Garlands and decorations
34. Волшебное заклинание (vol-SHEB-no-ye zak-LI-nan-ee-ye) - Magical spell

35. Время радости и веселья (VRYE-myah RA-dos-tee i vye-SE-lya) - Time for joy and merriment

36. Семейный ужин (se-MEY-nyy oo-ZHEEN) - Family dinner

37. Новогодний фейерверк (no-vo-GOD-nyy fye-er-VERK) - New Year fireworks

38. Украшенная елка (uk-ra-SHEn-na-ya YEL-ka) - Decorated Christmas tree

39. Приготовление праздничных блюд (pree-go-vo-lye-NYE praz-DEE-chnykh blyud) - Cooking festive dishes

40. Новогодний марафон фильмов (no-vo-GOD-nyy ma-ra-FON FEE-lmov) - New Year movie marathon

41. Популярные новогодние песни (po-poo-LYAR-ny-ye no-vo-GOD-ny-ye PE-snee) - Popular New Year songs

42. Подарочная упаковка (po-da-ROCH-na-ya oo-PA-ko-vka) - Gift wrapping

43. Встреча с Дедом Морозом (VSTRE-cha s DE-dom Mo-RO-zom) - Meeting with Santa Claus

44. Новогодний танец (no-vo-GOD-nyy TA-nyets) - New Year dance

45. Зимний праздничный наряд (ZIM-niy praz-DNEECH-nyy na-RYAD) - Winter festive attire

46. Новогоднее счастье (no-vo-GOD-nye shas-TYE) - New Year happiness

47. Новогодняя елочка (no-vo-GOD-ny-ya YEL-och-ka) - New Year tree

48. Романтический ужин при свечах (ro-man-TEE-skiy oo-ZHEEN pree SVE-cha) - Romantic candlelit dinner

49. Снежная битва (SNEZH-naya BEET-va) - Snowball fight

50. Зимний вечер у камина (ZIM-niy VYE-cher oo ka-MEE-na) - Winter evening by the fireplace

51. Подарок от Санта Клауса (po-da-ROK ot SAN-ta KLAU-sa) - Gift from Santa Claus

52. Ёлочные игрушки (YO-loch-nye ig-ROOSH-ki) - Christmas decorations

53. Волшебные сказки (vol-SHEB-nye S-KAZ-ki) - Magical fairy tales

54. Зимний карнавал (ZIM-niy kar-NA-val) - Winter carnival

55. Приятное общение с близкими (pri-YAT-no-ye ob-SCHYE-nye s BLEEZ-kee-mee)

USEFUL TELEPHONE PHRASES IN RUSSIAN

1. Алло? (AH-lo) - Hello? (Answering a call)

2. Здравствуйте (ZDRAST-vooy-tye) - Hello (Formal)

3. Привет (PREE-vyet) - Hi / Hello (Informal)

4. Кто говорит? (KTO ga-vo-REET) - Who is speaking?

5. Я говорю... (YA ga-vo-ryo...) - This is...

6. Я хотел бы поговорить с... (YA kho-TYEL by pa-ga-va-REET′ s...) - I would like to speak with...

7. Извините, но вы ошиблись номером (eez-vee-NEE-tye, no vy o-SHEE-blyis′ NO-mye-rom) - Sorry, but you have the wrong number.

8. Могу я поговорить с...? (MA-goo ya pa-ga-va-REET′ s...) - May I speak with...?

9. Я передам ваше сообщение (YA pye-RE-dam vash-ye so-BRASH-ye-nye) - I will pass along your message.

10. Подождите, пожалуйста (pa-da-ZHDI-tye, pa-ZHA-lus-ta) - Please hold on.

11. Конечно, я передам (ka-NECH-na, YA pye-RE-dam) - Of course, I will transfer you.

12. Ваш звонок очень важен для нас (vash ZVO-nok OTCHEN va-ZHEN DLYA nas) - Your call is important to us.

13. Мы перезвоним вам (my pye-REZ-vo-neem vam) - We will call you back.

14. Сейчас я свободен (SEY-chas ya sva-BO-dyen) - I am currently available.

15. Я не могу разобрать, что вы говорите (YA nye MA-gu ra-za-BRAT', chto vy ga-vo-REE-tye) - I can't understand what you're saying.

16. Прошу повторить еще раз (pra-shu paft-o-REET' YESH-cho ras) - Please repeat it again.

17. Не могли бы вы говорить громче? (nye MAG-lee by vy ga-vo-REET' grum-CHE) - Could you speak louder?

18. Извините, мне нужно отойти от телефона (eez-vee-NEE-tye, mnye NOOZH-na a-TUY-tee at tee-LEE-fo-NA) - Sorry, I need to step away from the phone.

19. Будьте добры, оставьте сообщение после сигнала (BOOT'-tye DOB-ry, a-stav'-tye so-BRASH-ye-nye pa-SLYE seeg-NA-la) - Please leave a message after the beep.

20. Спасибо за звонок (spa-SEE-ba za ZVO-nok) - Thank you for calling.

21. Чем могу помочь? (chem MA-goo pa-MOCH') - How can I help?

22. Это срочный звонок (EH-ta SROCH-ny ZVO-nok) - This is an urgent call.

23. Я хотел бы получить информацию о... (YA kho-TYEL by pa-LOO-chit' in-for-MA-tsee-yu a...) - I would like to get information about...

24. Можно задать вопрос? (MAZH-na za-DAT' va-PROS) - Can I ask a question?

25. Что случилось? (chto SLOO-chee-LAS') - What happened?

26. Я не могу связаться с... (YA nye MA-goo svi-ZA-tsya s...) - I can't reach...

27. Это номер для экстренных случаев (EH-ta NO-myer dlya eek-STREN-nykh SLOO-che-ev) - This is the emergency number.

28. У вас есть запись на...? (oo vas yest za-REES na...) - Do you have an appointment for...?

29. Пожалуйста, подтвердите вашу личность (pa-ZHA-lus-ta podt-VER-dy-tye va-SHOO leechnost') - Please confirm your identity.

30. Я передам ваш запрос ответственному лицу (YA pye-RE-dam vash za-PROS a-TYETS-tven-na-mu LEE-tsu) - I will forward your request to the responsible person.

31. Прошу вас подождать минутку (pra-SHU vas pa-da-ZHDAT' mee-NOOT-ku) - Please wait a moment.

32. Когда вам будет удобно? (KOHN-da vam BU-dyet oo-DOB-na) - When would it be convenient for you?

33. Извините за ожидание (eez-vee-NEE-tye za o-ZHID-a-nee-ye) - Sorry for the wait.

34. Я буду доступен после... (YA BOO-doo dost-oo-PYEN pa-S LE...) - I will be available after...

35. Ответьте на этот вопрос, пожалуйста (a-TVYET-tye na ETOT va-PROS pa-ZHA-lus-ta) - Please answer this question.

36. Я не могу сейчас ответить на этот вопрос (YA nye MA-goo SEY-chas ot-VET-eet' na ETOT va-PROS) - I can't answer that question right now.

37. Что я могу сказать по этому поводу? (chto ya MA-goo SKA-zat' pa ETOMU pa-VO-du) - What can I say about that?

38. Прошу вас продолжить (pra-SHU vas pra-DOL-zheet') - Please go on.

39. Извините, но я не могу помочь (eez-vee-NEE-tye, no YA nye MA-goo pa-MOCH') - Sorry, but I can't help.

40. Я передам вашу просьбу своему руководителю (YA pye-RE-dam va-SHOO PROS'-boo sva-VO-mu roo-ka-VEE-telyu)

41. Что вы хотите узнать? (chto vy KHO-tee-tye ooz-NAT') - What would you like to know?

42. Я проверю эту информацию для вас (YA pra-VE-ryu eta in-FOR-ma-tsee-YU dlya vas) - I will check this information for you.

43. Это работает круглосуточно (EH-ta ra-BA-ta-yet kroog-la-SOO-tach-na) - This operates 24/7.

44. Переведите меня к главному менеджеру (pye-RE-vee-DYE-tye mye-NYA k glav-NO-moo mye-nyed-ZYE-ru) - Transfer me to the manager.

45. Какой у вас номер телефона? (KA-koy oo vas NO-myer tee-le-FO-na) - What is your phone number?

46. Что делать, если утерян телефон? (chto dyelat', YES-lee oo-tye-RYAN tee-le-FON) - What to do if the phone is lost?

47. Извините за трудности (eez-vee-NEE-tye za TROOD-nos-tee) - Sorry for the inconvenience.

48. Это необходимо для безопасности (EH-ta nye-neh-DYE-ma dlya bYE-zo-pas-NO-stee) - This is necessary for security.

49. Понятно, я перезвоню позже (po-NYAT-na, YA pye-REZ-vo-nyu poZH-yeh) - Understand, I will call back later.

UKRAINIAN

1. She visits her father.

Вона відвідує свого батька.

1. I call telephone my friend.   Дзвоню подрузі.

2. I travel a lot.   Я багато подорожую.

3. I have a lemon.   У мене є лимон.

OO mene ye lee-mon

5. I have a melon.   У мене є диня.

Oo mene ye dyna.

6. You take two oranges.

Ви берете два апельсини.   Vy berete dvacapelsyny.

7. I like tomatoes.

Я люблю помідори.

Meni podobayutsya pomidory.

8. I don't like beans.   Я не люблю квасолю.

Meni nye podobayutsya boby.

9. I don't like onions.   Я не люблю цибулю.

Ya nye lyublyou tsee-boo-lee.

10. I drink.   я п′ю   Ya pyou

11. I drink juice.   Я п′ю сік.   Ya pyou sik

12. You drink.   Ви п′єте. Ty pyesh.

13. You drink water.   Ви п′єте воду.

Ty pyesh vah-doo

14. They drink   Вони п′ють   Vah-nee pyout.

15. They drink water and juice.   П′ють воду і сік.

Vah-nee pyout vah-doo ee sik.

16. You make tea.   Ви заварюєте чай.

Tee robeesh chay.

17. I drink water with ice.   Я п′ю воду з льодом.

Yah pyou vah-doo z lyodom.

18. He would like black coffee.   Він хоче чорної кави. Vin hotiv by chor-noo kah-voo.

19. She would like milk.   Вона хоче молока.

Vah-nah b hoteelah molokah.

20. I'm eating a sandwich.   Я їм бутерброд.

Yah yim sendvich.

21. I'm eating a sanwich with cheese.

Я їм бутерброд з сиром.

Yah yim booter-brot z syrom.

22. I take a piece of bread.   Я беру шматок хліба.

Yah beroo shmah-tok hliba.

23. We take two pieces of cheese. Ми Беремо два шматочки сиру.

My beremo dva shmahtahchkee syroo.

24. Do you have fish?   У вас є риба.

Oo vas ye ryba?

25. Where is the salt?   Де сіль?   Day seel?

26. Can you bring me a fork?

Ви можете принести мені виделку?

Mozhete preenestee menee veedyel-koo?

27. Can you bring me a spoon?

Можеш принести мені ложку?

Mozhete preenestee meni lozh-koo?

28. Do you have a city map? У вас є карта міста?

Oo vahs ye kahr-tah mees-tah?

29. Where is the post office? Де пошта? Dye posh-tah?

30. Where is the pharmacy? Де знаходиться аптека? Dye znah-hoteetsyah ahp-tyekah?

31. We need rice and bread. Нам потрібні рис і хліб. Nshm po-tree-ben rees ee hleep

32. We need tomatoes for the soup. Для супу нам знадоблятся помідори.

Nahm po-treeb-nee po-mee-doree dlyah soopoo.

33. Where is the grocery store? Де знаходиться супермаркет? Dye znah-ho-deetsyah

Sooper-marhket. Or Dye ye sooper-market?

34. Where is the market? Де знаходиться ринок? De znahodytsa bahzar?

35. Do you sell fruits and vegetables? Ви продаєте фрукти та овочі?

Chee vee prodayete frooktee tah ovahchee?

36. We sell fruits and vegetables. Продаємо фрукти та овочі.

My prodayyemo frootee tah o-vah-chee.

37. I have to buy a book. Я маю купити книжку. Ya may-you koopeetee kneezhkoo.

38. I have to go to the bookstore. Мені потрібно піти в книгарню. Menee potreebnah eetee v knoo-harn-you.

39. I have to go to the supermarket. Мені потрібно піти в супермаркет.

Menee pahtreeb-nah eetee v sooper-mahr-ket.

Useful Ukrainian Phrases

1. Привіт! (Pryvit!) - Hello!
2. Дякую! (Dyakuyu!) - Thank you!
3. Вибачте! (Vybachte!) - Excuse me!
4. Так (Tak) - Yes
5. Ні (Ni) - No
6. Будь ласка (Bud' laska) - Please
7. Як справи? (Yak spravy?) - How are you?
8. Я не розумію. (Ya ne rozumiyu.) - I don't understand.
9. Де знаходиться...? (De znakhodyt'sya...?) - Where is...?
10. Скільки це коштує? (Skil'ky tse koshtuye?) - How much does this cost?
11. Я говорю англійською. (Ya hovoryu anhliyskoyu.) - I speak English.
12. Дуже приємно! (Duzhe priemno!) - Nice to meet you!
13. Мене звуть... (Mene zvut'...) - My name is...
14. Я вас не розумію. (Ya vas ne rozumiyu.) - I don't understand you.
15. Допоможіть, будь ласка. (Dopomoʒitʲ, budʹ laska.) - Help me, please.
16. Як вас звати? (Yak vas zvaty?) - What is your name?
17. Я з... (Ya z...) - I am from...

18. Доброго дня! (Dobroho dnya!) - Good day!

19. Простите! (Prostite!) - I'm sorry!

20. До побачення! (Do pobachennya!) - Goodbye!

21. Я вдячний! (Ya vdyachnyy!) - I am grateful!

22. Я не знаю. (Ya ne znayu.) - I don't know.

23. Що робити? (Shcho robyty?) - What to do?

24. Ви розмовляєте англійською? (Vy rozmovlyayete anhliyskoyu?) - Do you speak English?

25. Чим можу допомогти? (Chym mozhy dopomohty?) - How can I help?

26. Де туалет? (De tualet?) - Where is the toilet?

27. Я голодний/голодна. (Ya holodnyy/holodna.) - I am hungry.

28. Я хочу пити. (Ya khochu pyty.) - I want to drink.

29. Я втомився/втомилася. (Ya vtomyvsya/vtomylasya.) - I am tired.

30. Я радий/рада. (Ya radyy/rada.) - I am happy.

31. Дякую за все. (Dyakuyu za vse.) - Thank you for everything.

32. Я вас люблю. (Ya vas lyublyu.) - I love you.

33. Добрий ранок! (Dobryy ranok!) - Good morning!

34. Добрий вечір! (Dobryy vechir!) - Good evening!

35. Я слухаю музику. (Ya slukhayu muzyku.) - I am listening to music.

36. Я дивлюся телевізор. (Ya dyvlyusya televizor.) - I am watching TV.

37. Я читаю книжку. (Ya chytayu knyzhku.) - I am reading a book.

38. Я йду додому. (Ya ydu dodomu.) - I am going home.

39. Де ви живете? (De vy zhyvete?) - Where do you live?

40. Я зайнятий/зайнята. (Ya zaynyatyy/zaynyata.) - I am busy.

41. Я вчусь університеті. (Ya vchus' universyteti.) - I study at the university.

42. Я хочу відпочити. (Ya khochu vidpochyty.) - I want to relax.

43. Я хочу зустрітися з друзями. (Ya khochu zustritysya z druzhyami.) - I want to meet with friends.

44. Добро пожаловать! (Dobro pozhalovat'!) - Welcome!

45. Я зголоднів/зголодніла. (Ya zgolodniv/zgolodnila.) - I got hungry.

46. Я готовий/готова. (Ya gotovyy/gotova.) - I am ready.

47. Я не згоден/згодна. (Ya ne zhoden/zhodna.) - I disagree.

48. Я погоджуюся. (Ya pogodzhuyusya.) - I agree.

49. До скорої зустрічі! (Do skoroyi zustrichi!) - See you soon!

50. Я це люблю! (Ya tse lyublyu!) - I love it!

USEFUL BUSINESS UKRAINIAN PHRASES

1. Дуже приємно познайомитися. (Duzhe pryiemno poznaiomytysia.) - Nice to meet you.

2. Будь ласка. (Bud' laska.) - Please.

3. Дякую. (Diakuiu.) - Thank you.

4. Дуже вдячний/вдячна. (Duzhe vdachnyi/vdachna.) - I am very grateful.

5. Пробачте. (Probachte.) - Excuse me.

6. Що можу для вас зробити? (Shcho mozu dlia vas zrobyty?) - What can I do for you?

7. Погодьтеся. (Pohod"tesia.) - Agreed.

8. Перепрошую за затримку. (Pereproshuiu za zatrymku.) - Sorry for the delay.

9. Чи можна задати питання? (Chy mozhna zadaty pytannia?) - May I ask a question?

10. Я рекомендую... (Ya rekomenduiu...) - I recommend...

11. Де знаходиться...? (De znakhodyt'sia...?) - Where is... located?

12. Я хотів би замовити... (Ya khotiv by zamovyty...) - I would like to order...

13. Це найкращий вибір. (Tse naikrashchyi vybir.) - It's the best choice.

14. Дуже цікаво. (Duzhe tsikavo.) - Very interesting.

15. Які ваші умови? (Yaki vashi umovy?) - What are your terms?

16. Це дороге. (Tse drohe.) - It's expensive.

17. У вас є гуртові знижки? (U vas ye hurtovi znyzhky?) - Do you have wholesale discounts?

18. Це можна повернути? (Tse mozhna povernuty?) - Can this be returned?

19. Які у вас методи оплати? (Yaki u vas metody oplaty?) - What payment methods do you have?

20. Я не згоден. (Ya ne zghoden.) - I disagree.

21. Ви готові до співпраці? (Vy hotovi do spivpratsi?) - Are you ready to cooperate?

22. Я радий співпрацювати з вами. (Ya radyi spivpratsiuvaty z vamy.) - I'm glad to cooperate with you.

23. Ваші товари чудові. (Vashi tovary chudovi.) - Your products are excellent.

24. Я розумію. (Ya rozumiiu.) - I understand.

25. Сподіваюся на плідну співпрацю. (Spodivaiusia na plidnu spivpratsiu.) - I hope for fruitful cooperation.

26. Я впевнений у цьому. (Ya vpevnenyi u ts'omu.) - I am confident in this.

27. Ви отримаєте знижку. (Vy otrymat'e znyzhku.) - You'll receive a discount.

28. Це недорого. (Tse nedoroho.) - It's inexpensive.

29. Який ваш графік роботи? (Yakyi vash hrafik roboty?) - What is your working schedule?

30. Це занизена ціна. (Tse zanyzena tsina.) - It's a discounted price.

31. Допоможіть мені, будь ласка. (Dopomozhit' meni, bud' laska.) - Help me, please.

32. Якщо ви згодні... (Yakshcho vy zghodni...) - If you agree...

33. Буде радість знову побачитися. (Bude radiist' znovu pobachytysia.) - It will be a pleasure to see you again.

34. Ваша пропозиція цікава. (Vasha propozytsiia tsikava.) - Your offer is interesting.

35. Це велика угода. (Tse velyka uhoda.) - It's a great deal.

36. Вітаю з успішним виконанням. (Viitaiu z uspishnym vykonanniam.) - Congratulations on the successful completion.

37. Це не підходить. (Tse ne pidkhodyt'.) - This doesn't suit.

38. Як давно ви на ринку? (Yak davno vy na rynku?) - How long have you been on the market?

39. Повідомте мене, будь ласка. (Povidomte mene, bud' laska.) - Please inform me.

40. Ми обов'язково з вами зв'яжемося. (My obov'yazkovo z vamy zv"iazhemosiia.) - We will definitely get in touch with you.

41. Термін доставки - два дні. (Termin dostavky - dva dni.) - Delivery time is two days.

42. Можна отримати знижку? (Mozhna otrymaty znyzhku?) - Can I get a discount?

43. Все просто чудово. (Vse prosto chudovo.) - Everything is simply wonderful.

44. Мої вітання з цим досягненням. (Moii vitannia z tsym dosiahnenniam.) - Congratulations on this achievement.

45. Якщо виникнуть питання, будь ласка, зверніться до нас. (Yakshcho vynyknut' pytannia, bud' laska, zvernit'sia do nas.) - If you have any questions, please contact us.

46. Це необхідно врахувати. (Tse neobkhidno vrakhuvaty.) - It needs to be taken into account.

47. Чи можна отримати дисконтну картку? (Chy mozhna otrymaty dyskontnu kartku?) - Can I get a discount card?

48. Якщо потрібна допомога, зверніться до нас. (Yakshcho potribna dopomoha, zvernit'sia do nas.) - If you need help, please contact us.

49. Ви відрізняєтесь високою якістю. (Vy vidrizniaietesia vysokoiu yakistiu.) - You stand out for your high quality.

50. Я сподіваюсь на подальшу співпрацю. (Ya spodivaius

USEFUL AIRPORT UKRAINIAN PHRASES

1. Міжнародний аеропорт. (Mizhnarodnyi aeroport.) - International airport.
2. Літак. (Litak.) - Airplane.
3. Приземлення. (Pryzemlennia.) - Landing.
4. Вильот. (Vylot.) - Departure.
5. Прильот. (Prylot.) - Arrival.
6. Кіоск преси. (Kiosk presy.) - Newsstand.
7. Багаж. (Bahazh.) - Luggage.
8. Паспортний контроль. (Pasportnyi kontrol'.) - Passport control.
9. Охорона. (Okhorona.) - Security.
10. Посадковий квиток. (Posadkovyj kvytok.) - Boarding pass.
11. Сканування багажу. (Skannuvannia bahazhu.) - Baggage scanning.
12. Митний контроль. (Mytnyi kontrol'.) - Customs control.
13. Авіакомпанія. (Aviakompaniia.) - Airline.
14. Служба пасажирських оголошень. (Sluzhba pasazhyrskykh oholoshen'.) - Passenger announcements.
15. Рейс. (Reis.) - Flight.
16. Вихід. (Vykhid.) - Exit.

17. Зона безмитного товару. (Zona bezmytnoho tovaru.) - Duty-free zone.

18. Рентген-сканування. (Renthen-skannuvannia.) - X-ray scanning.

19. Реєстрація пасажирів. (Reiestratsiia pasazhyriv.) - Passenger check-in.

20. Аеропортовий персонал. (Aeroportovyi personal.) - Airport staff.

21. Каса. (Kasa.) - Cashier.

22. Транзит. (Tranzyt.) - Transit.

23. Безпека. (Bezpeka.) - Security.

24. Запитання. (Zapytannia.) - Questions.

25. Посадка в літак. (Posadka v litak.) - Boarding the plane.

26. Затримка. (Zatrymka.) - Delay.

27. Компанія з оренди автомобілів. (Kompaniia z orendy avtomobiliv.) - Car rental company.

28. Безкоштовний Wi-Fi. (Bezkoshtovnyi Wi-Fi.) - Free Wi-Fi.

29. Диванчики для відпочинку. (Divanchyky dlia vidpochynku.) - Lounge seating.

30. Вітальний зал. (Vital'nyi zal.) - Arrival hall.

31. Пасажирський ліфт. (Pasazhyrskyi lift.) - Passenger elevator.

32. Рейсовий інформатор. (Reisovyi informator.) - Flight information display.

33. Безкоштовний автобус. (Bezkoshtovnyi avtobus.) - Free shuttle bus.

34. Телефонів прокат. (Telefoniv prokat.) - Phone rental.

35. Природний сік. (Pryrodnyi sik.) - Natural juice.

36. Кафе. (Kafe.) - Café.

37. Міжнародний рейс. (Mizhnarodnyi reis.) - International flight.

38. Пасажирські сходи. (Pasazhyrski skhody.) - Passenger stairs.

39. Справочна служба. (Spravochna sluzhba.) - Information service.

40. Банкомат. (Bankomat.) - ATM.

41. Вартість авіаквитків. (Vartist aviakvytkiv.) - Airfare.

42. Автоматичне оголошення. (Avtomatychne oholoshennia.) - Automated announcement.

43. Затримка рейсу. (Zatrymka reisu.) - Flight delay.

44. Особливі потреби. (Osoblyvi potreby.) - Special needs.

45. Безпечне вилітне лунк. (Bezpechne vylitne lunok.) - Secure departure gate.

46. Туристичне агентство. (Turystychne ahentsvo.) - Travel agency.

47. Зона очікування. (Zona ochikuvannia.) - Waiting area.

48. Пасажирський транспорт. (Pasazhyrskyi transport.) - Passenger transport.

49. Безкоштовні тележки. (Bezkoshtovni telezhky.) - Free luggage carts.

50. Пункт обміну валют. (Punkt obminu valiut.) - Currency exchange point.

Numbers in Ukrainian

1 - один (oh-deen)
2 - два (dva)
3 - три (tree)
4 - чотири (cho-ty-ri)
5 - п'ять (p'yat')
6 - шість (shist')
7 - сім (sim)
8 - вісім (vi-sim)
9 - дев'ять (dev'yat')
10 - десять (deh-syat')
11 - одинадцять (oh-dy-na-dz'yat')
12 - дванадцять (dva-na-dz'yat')
13 - тринадцять (try-na-dz'yat')
14 - чотирнадцять (cho-tyr-na-dz'yat')
15 - п'ятнадцять (p'yat-na-dz'yat')
16 - шістнадцять (shist-na-dz'yat')
17 - сімнадцять (sim-na-dz'yat')
18 - вісімнадцять (vi-sim-na-dz'yat')
19 - дев'ятнадцять (dev'yat-na-dz'yat')
20 - двадцять (dva-dz'yat')
21 - двадцять один (dva-dz'yat' oh-deen)

22 - двадцять два (dva-dz′yat′ dva)

23 - двадцять три (dva-dz′yat′ tree)

24 - двадцять чотири (dva-dz′yat′ cho-ty-ri)

25 - двадцять п'ять (dva-dz′yat′ p′yat′)

26 - двадцять шість (dva-dz′yat′ shist′)

27 - двадцять сім (dva-dz′yat′ sim)

28 - двадцять вісім (dva-dz′yat′ vi-sim)

29 - двадцять дев'ять (dva-dz′yat′ dev′yat′)

30 - тридцять (try-dz′yat′)

31 - тридцять один (try-dz′yat′ oh-deen)

32 - тридцять два (try-dz′yat′ dva)

33 - тридцять три (try-dz′yat′ tree)

34 - тридцять чотири (try-dz′yat′ cho-ty-ri)

35 - тридцять п'ять (try-dz′yat′ p′yat′)

36 - тридцять шість (try-dz′yat′ shist′)

37 - тридцять сім (try-dz′yat′ sim)

38 - тридцять вісім (try-dz′yat′ vi-sim)

39 - тридцять дев'ять (try-dz′yat′ dev′yat′)

40 - сорок (so-rok)

41 - сорок один (so-rok oh-deen)

42 - сорок два (so-rok dva)

43 - сорок три (so-rok tree)

44 - сорок чотири (so-rok cho-ty-ri)

45 - сорок п'ять (so-rok p′yat′)

46 - сорок шість (so-rok shist′)

47 - сорок сім (so-rok sim)

48 - сорок вісім (so-rok vi-sim)

49 - сорок дев'ять (so-rok dev′yat′)

50 - п'ятдесят (p′yat-deh-syat′)

51 - п'ятдесят один (p′yat-deh-syat′ oh-deen)

52 - п'ятдесят два (p'yat-deh-syat' dva)
53 - п'ятдесят три (p'yat-deh-syat' tree)
54 - п'ятдесят чотири (p'yat-deh-syat' cho-ty-ri)
55 - п'ятдесят п'ять (p'yat-deh-syat' p'yat')
56 - п'ятдесят шість (p'yat-deh-syat' shist')
57 - п'ятдесят сім (p'yat-deh-syat' sim)
58 - п'ятдесят вісім (p'yat-deh-syat' vi-sim)
59 - п'ятдесят дев'ять (p'yat-deh-syat' dev'yat')
60 - шістдесят (shist-deh-syat')
61 - шістдесят один (shist-deh-syat' oh-deen)
62 - шістдесят два (shist-deh-syat' dva)
63 - шістдесят три (shist-deh-syat' tree)
64 - шістдесят чотири (shist-deh-syat' cho-ty-ri)
65 - шістдесят п'ять (shist-deh-syat' p'yat')
66 - шістдесят шість (shist-deh-syat' shist')
67 - шістдесят сім (shist-deh-syat' sim)
68 - шістдесят вісім (shist-deh-syat' vi-sim)
69 - шістдесят дев'ять (shist-deh-syat' dev'yat')
70 - сімдесят (sim-deh-syat')
71 - сімдесят один (sim-deh-syat' oh-deen)
72 - сімдесят два (sim-deh-syat' dva)
73 - сімдесят три (sim-deh-syat' tree)
74 - сімдесят чотири (sim-deh-syat' cho-ty-ri)
75 - сімдесят п'ять (sim-deh-syat' p'yat')
76 - сімдесят шість (sim-deh-syat' shist')
77 - сімдесят сім (sim-deh-syat' sim)
78 - сімдесят вісім (sim-deh-syat' vi-sim)
79 - сімдесят дев'ять (sim-deh-syat' dev'yat')
80 - вісімдесят (vi-sim-deh-syat')
81 - вісімдесят один (vi-sim-deh-syat' oh-deen)

82 - вісімдесят два (vi-sim-deh-syat′ dva)
83 - вісімдесят три (vi-sim-deh-syat′ tree)
84 - вісімдесят чотири (vi-sim-deh-syat′ cho-ty-ri)
85 - вісімдесят п'ять (vi-sim-deh-syat′ p′yat′)
86 - вісімдесят шість (vi-sim-deh-syat′ shist′)
87 - вісімдесят сім (vi-sim-deh-syat′ sim)

USEUL POSTAL UKRAINIAN PHRASES

1. Добрий день. (Dobryy den') - Good day.

2. Я бажаю надіслати цей лист до... (Ya bah-zhah-yu nad-y-slah-ty tsey list do...) - I would like to send this letter to...

3. Скільки коштує відправити цей пакунок? (Skil'ky ko-shtoo-ye vi-dpra-vy-ty tsey pa-koon-ok?) - How much does it cost to send this package?

4. Де знаходиться найближче поштове відділення? (De zna-ko-dee-t'sya nai-blyzh-che po-sh-to-ve vid-i-lyen-nya?) - Where is the nearest post office located?

5. Чи можна отримати стягнення при доставці? (Chy mo-zna o-try-ma-ty st-YAHHN-yen-nya pri dos-tav-tsi?) - Can I receive a collection upon delivery?

6. Можна подати заявку на одержання? (Mo-zhna po-da-ty za-yav-ku na o-der-zhan-nya?) - Can I file a request for receiving?

7. Чи є трекінг-номер для цієї посилки? (Chy ye trek-kinh nom-er dla tsyi pos-il-ki?) - Is there a tracking number for this shipment?

8. Як довго триває доставка в мій регіон? (Yak doh-voh try-vah-ye dos-tav-ka v mii reh-gyon?) - How long does delivery take to my region?

9. Потрібен штамп платникам на цій поштовій марці. (Po-tri-ben shtamp plat-ny-kaam na tsii posh-to-vii mart-see) - A stamp is required for payment on this postal mark.

10. Чи є каса для оплати послуг у вашому відділенні? (Chy ye ka-sa dla o-pla-ty pos-looh u vaa-sho-moo vid-i-lyen-nee?) - Is there a cash desk for service payment at your branch?

USEFUL TELEPHONE PHRASES IN UKRAINIAN

1. Добрий день. (Dobry den') - Good day.

2. Привіт. (Pryvit) - Hello.

3. Здрастуйте. (Zdrastuyte) - Greetings.

4. Я хотів би поспілкуватися з... (Ya hotiv by pospilkuvasya z...) - I would like to speak with...

5. Чи можу я поговорити з... (Chy mohu ya pohovoryty z...) - May I speak with...

6. Це номер... (Tse nomer...) - This is the number...

7. Хто питає? (Khto pytae?) - Who is calling?

8. Я зателефонував щодо... (Ya zatelefonuvav shchodo...) - I'm calling about...

9. Я хотів(-ла) би записати повідомлення. (Ya hotiv(-la) by zapysaty povidomlennya) - I would like to leave a message.

10. Чи можете ви передзвонити пізніше? (Chy mozhete vy peredzvonity piznishe?) - Can you call back later?

11. Я шукаю контактний номер/інформацію. (Ya shukayu kontaktyny nomer/informatsiyu) - I'm looking for a contact number/information.

12. Чи є у вас номер для технічної підтримки? (Chy ye u vas nomer dlya tekhnichnoyi pidtrymky?) - Do you have a technical support number?

13. Я хотів би дізнатися години роботи компанії. (Ya hotiv by diznatysya hodyny roboty kompaniyi) - I would like to know the company's working hours.

14. Ви можете дати мені інформацію про ваші послуги/продукти? (Vy mozhete dati meni informatsiyu pro vashi poslugy/produkti?) - Can you give me information about your services/products?

15. Чи є у вас вакансії? (Chy ye u vas vakansiyi?) - Do you have any job vacancies?

16. Чи можете ви передати повідомлення? (Chy mozhete vy peredaty povidomlennya?) - Can you take a message?

17. Чи є у вас номер готелю/ресторану/магазину? (Chy ye u vas nomer hotelyu/restoranu/mahazynu?) - Do you have the number for a hotel/restaurant/shop?

18. Я бажаю з'ясувати інформацію про оплату. (Ya bazhahu z'yasuvaty informatsiyu pro oplatu) - I wish to inquire about payment information.

19. Чи можете ви мені допомогти з проблемою? (Chy mozhete vy meni dopomogty z problemoyu?) - Can you help me with an issue?

20. Чи можете ви пояснити цю процедуру більш детально? (Chy mozhete vy poyasnity tsyu protseduru bil'sh detalyno?) - Can you explain this procedure in more detail?

21. Я заблокував мій акаунт. (Ya zablokuvav moyi akkaunt) - I've locked my account.

22. Чи можете ви скинути моє пароль? (Chy mozhete vy skynuty moye parol?) - Can you reset my password?

23. Я не можу отримати доступ до мого електронного листа. (Ya ne mozhy otrymaty dostup do mogo elektronnoho lysta) - I can't access my email.

24. Чи можете ви дати мені підказку для відновлення пароля? (Chy mozhete vy dati meni pidkazku dlya vidnovlennya parolya?) - Can you give me a hint to recover my password?

25. Я хотів (-ла) би запланувати зустріч. (Ya hotiv (-la) by zaplanuvaty zustrich) - I would like to schedule a meeting.

26. Чи можете ви надіслати мені деталі за цей рахунок? (Chy mozhete vy nadislaty meni detali za tsey rakhunok?) - Can you send me the details for this invoice?

27. Чи можете ви підтвердити, що отримали мою оплату? (Chy mozhete vy pidtverdyty, shcho otrymaly moyu oplatu?) - Can you confirm that you've received my payment?

28. Я хотів (-ла) би змінити мою адресу електронної пошти. (Ya hotiv (-la) by zminyty moyu adresu elektronnoyi poshti) - I would like to change my email address.

29. Чи є у вас акційна пропозиція на даний момент? (Chy ye u vas aktsiyna propozytsiya na danyy moment?) - Do you have any current promotional offers?

30. Я хотів (-ла) би замовити продукт/послугу. (Ya hotiv (-la) by zamovyty produkt/poslugu) - I would like to order a product/service.

31. Чи можете ви надіслати мені інформацію електронною поштою? (Chy mozhete vy nadislaty meni informatsiyu elektronnoyu poshtoiu?) - Can you send me information via email?

32. Чи є у вас гарантія на цей продукт? (Chy ye u vas garantiya na tsey produkt?) - Do you provide a warranty for this product?

33. Я хотів бы забронировать номер на определенную дату. (Ya hotiv by zareservuvaty nomer na optymal'nu datu) - I would like to book a room for a specific date.

34. Чи можете ви затримати доставку на кілька днів? (Chy mozhete vy zatrymaty dostavku na kil'ka dniv?) - Can you delay the delivery by a few days?

35. Чи можете ви надати мені назву і номер вашого менеджера? (Chy mozhete vy nadaty meni nazvu i nomer vashogo menedzhera?) - Can you provide me with the name and number of your manager?

36. Чи можна отримати довідку про ваші послуги/продукти? (Chy mozhna otrymaty dovidku pro vashi poslugy/produkti?) - Can I get a brochure about your services/products?

37. Я хотів (-ла) би отримати допомогу з встановленням програмного забезпечення. (Ya hotiv (-la) by otrymaty dopomohu z vstanovlennyam prohramnoho zabespechennya) - I would like assistance with software installation.

38. Чи можна отримати копію рахунку? (Chy mozhna otrymaty kopiyu rakhunku?) - Can I get a copy of the bill?

39. Чи є у вас послуга доставки на місце? (Chy ye u vas posluga dostavky na mistse?) - Do you offer on-site delivery service?

40. Чи можна оплатити замовлення онлайн? (Chy mozhna oplatyty zamovlennya onlayn?) - Can I pay for the order online?

41. Чи є у вас розширені години роботи? (Chy ye u vas rozshyreni hodyny roboty?) - Do you have extended working hours?

42. Чи можете ви пояснити, як користуватися вашим продуктом/сервісом? (Chy mozhete vy poyasnity, yak korystuvatysya vashym produktom/ser,isom?) - Can you explain how to use your product/service?

43. Я хотів бы перенести зустріч на інший день. (Ya hotiv by perenesty zustrich na inshyy den') - I would like to reschedule the meeting to another day.

44. Чи можна отримати підтвердження мого заказу? (Chy mozhna otrymaty pidtverdzhennya moho zamovlennya?) - Can I get confirmation of my order?

45. Чи маєте ви можливість забезпечити експрес-доставку? (Chy mayete vy mozhlyvist' zabespechyty ekspres-dostavku?) - Do you offer express delivery?

46. Чи є у вас можливість обслуговування на інших мовах? (Chy ye u vas mozhlyvist' obslugovuvannya na inshykh movakh?) - Do you provide service in other languages?

47. Я хотів бы відкласти час доставки. (Ya hotiv by vidklasty chas dostavky) - I would like to postpone the delivery time.

48. Чи можете ви роз'яснити умови гарантії? (Chy mozhete vy roz'yasnyty umovy garantiyi?) - Can you explain the terms of the warranty?

49. Чи можете ви надати мені додаткову інформацію щодо мого запиту? (Chy mozhete vy nadaty meni dodatkovu informatsiyu shchodo moho zapytu?) - Can you provide me with additional information regarding my inquiry?

50. Я хотів (-ла) би вжити заходів щодо скарги. (Ya hotiv (-la) by vzhyty zakhodiv shchodo skargy) - I would like to take steps regarding a complaint.

USEFUL HOLIDAY UKRAINIAN PHRASES

1. З Новим роком! (Z Novym rokom!) - Happy New Year!
2. Різдво з вами! (Rizdvo z vamy!) - Merry Christmas!
3. Веселих свят! (Veselykh svyat!) - Happy holidays!
4. Нехай ваші мрії збудуться! (Nekhay vashi mriyi zbudutsya!) - May your dreams come true!
5. Зичу вам щастя і здоров'я! (Zichu vam shchastya i zdorov'ya!) - I wish you happiness and good health!
6. Смачного святкового столу! (Smachnoho sviatkovoho stolu!) - Enjoy the festive table!
7. Успіхів у новому році! (Uspikhiv u novomu rotsi!) - Success in the new year!
8. Нехай наступний рік буде кращим! (Nekhay nastupnyy rik bude krashchym!) - May the next year be better!
9. Нехай щастя заполонить ваше життя! (Nekhay shchastya zapolonyt' vashe zhyttya!) - May happiness fill your life!
10. Щиро вітаю зі святами! (Shchyro vitayu zi sviatamy!) - Sincere congratulations on the holidays!
11. Здоров'я, радості та успіхів у новому році! (Zdorov'ya, radosti ta uspikhiv u novomu rotsi!) - Health, joy, and success in the new year!

12. Нехай Різдво принесе вам безліч радості! (Nekhay Rizdvo prynese vam bezlich radosti!) - May Christmas bring you abundant joy!

13. Нехай веселі моменти збагатять ваші свята! (Nekhay veseli momenty zbahaityat' vashi svyata!) - May joyful moments enrich your holidays!

14. Зичу вам спокою та гармонії на цих святкових днях. (Zichu vam spokoyu ta harmoniyi na tsikh sviatkovykh dnyah.) - I wish you peace and harmony during these festive days.

15. Нехай ваші серця будуть наповнені любов'ю цього Різдва. (Nekhay vashi sertsya bude napovnenni lyubov'yú ts'oho Rizdva.) - May your hearts be filled with love this Christmas.

16. Щиро дякую за вашу дружбу та підтримку протягом цього року. (Shyro dyakuyu za vashu druzhbu ta pidtrymku protyahom ts'oho roku.) - Thank you sincerely for your friendship and support throughout this year.

17. Бажаю вам веселих свят і яскравої зірки на небі. (Bazhayu vam veselykh svyat i yaskravoyi zirky na nebi.) - I wish you joyful holidays and a bright star in the sky.

18. Нехай ця зима принесе вам тепло та затишок. (Nekhay tsya zyma prynese vam teplo ta zatyshok.) - May this winter bring you warmth and coziness.

19. Зичу вам безліч усмішок та радості цього святкового сезону. (Zichu vam bezlich usmishok ta radosti ts'oho sviatkovoho sezonu.) - I wish you plenty of smiles and joy this holiday season.

20. Щиро вітаю з Різдвом Христовим! (Shchyro vitayu z Rizdvom Khrystovym!) - Warm wishes for Christmas!

21. Радості й щастя у новому році! (Radosti y shchastya u novomu rotsi!) - Joy and happiness in the new year!

22. Нехай Різдво ознаменує новий початок і нові можливості. (Nekhay Rizdvo oznamenuye novyy pochatok i novi mozhlyvosti.) - May Christmas mark a new beginning and new opportunities.

23. Зичу вам світлих і теплих свят! (Zichu vam svitlykh i teplykh svyat!) - I wish you bright and warm holidays!

24. Нехай кожна ваша мить буде наповнена радістю та любов'ю. (Nekhay kozhna vasha myt' bude napovnena radosky ta lyubov'yú.) - May every moment of yours be filled with joy and love.

25. Щиро вітаю з Різдвом! Нехай воно принесе вам безліч щастя та радості. (Shchyro vitayu z Rizdvom! Nekhay vono prynese vam bezlich shchastya ta radosti.) - Warm wishes for Christmas! May it bring you abundant happiness and joy.

26. Нехай ці свята наповнять ваші серця вірою й надією. (Nekhay tsi svyata napovnyat' vashi sertsya viroyu y nadiyeyu.) - May these holidays fill your hearts with faith and hope.

27. Зичу вам море позитивних емоцій цього чарівного періоду. (Zichu vam more pozityvnykh emotsiy ts'oho charivnoho periodu.) - I wish you an abundance of positive emotions during this magical time.

28. Хай свято Різдва приносить вам світло й тепло. (Khay sviato Rizdva prynosyt' vam svitlo y teplo.) - May the Christmas holiday bring you light and warmth.

29. Зичу вам благополуччя та достаток у новому році. (Zichu vam blahopoluchchya ta dostatok u novomu rotsi.) - I wish you prosperity and abundance in the new year.

30. Нехай новорічні мрії збуваються, а святкові дзвони радують ваші вушка. (Nekhay novorichni mriyi zbuva-yut'sya, a sviatkovi dzvony raduyut' vashi vushka.) - May New Year's dreams come true, and holiday bells bring joy to your ears.

31. Щасливих свят та веселе Різдво! (Shchaslyvykh svyat ta vesele Rizdvo!) - Happy holidays and Merry Christmas!

32. Зичу вам радості, затишку та щедрих дарунків. (Zichu vam radosti, zatyshku ta shchedrykh darunkiv.) - I wish you joy, comfort, and generous gifts.

33. Нехай святковий настрій не залишить вас цілий рік! (Nekhay svyatkovy nastriy ne zalishyt' vas tsilyy rik!) - May the holiday spirit stay with you all year round!

34. Зичу вам магічного Різдва, наповненого радістю та любов'ю. (Zichu vam mahichnogo Rizdva, napovnenogo radistyu ta liubov'yu.) - I wish you a magical Christmas filled with joy and love.

35. Щастя, любов та здійснення бажань - це мої побажання для вас! (Shchastya, lyubov ta zdiysnennya bazhan' - tse moyi pobazhannya dlya vas!) - Happiness, love, and fulfillment of wishes - these are my wishes for you!

36. Нехай кожний день святкового сезону буде повний нових вражень! (Nekhay kozhnyy den' sviatkovoho sezonu bude povnyy novykh vrazhen'!) - May each day of the holiday season be filled with new experiences!

37. Зичу вам чудесного Різдва, щедрого Діда Мороза та веселого святкового настрою. (Zichu vam chudesnoho Rizdva, shchedroho Dida Moroza ta veseloho sviatkovoho nastroyu.) - I wish you a wonderful Christmas, a generous Santa Claus, and a joyful holiday spirit.

38. Нехай магія Різдва подарує вам незабутні моменти з родиною та друзями. (Nekhay mahiya Rizdva podaruye vam nezabutni momenti z rodynoyu ta druzhamy.) - May the magic of Christmas bring you unforgettable moments with family and friends.

39. Зичу вам тепла, усмішок та надії, від яких свята стають яскравішими. (Zichu vam tepla, usmishok ta nadiyi, vid yakykh sviata stayut' yaskravishymy.) - I wish you warmth, smiles, and hope that make the holidays brighter.

40. Щирі побажання з окремим словом вдячності за вашу підтримку! (Shchiri pobazhannya z okremym slovom vdachnosti za vashu pidtrymku!) - Sincere wishes with a special word of gratitude for your support!

41. Нехай Різдво принесе вам море радості та щастя. (Nekhay Rizdvo prynese vam more radosti ta shchastya.) - May Christmas bring you a sea of joy and happiness.

42. Бажаю вам яскравого нового року, наповненого великими перемогами та незабутніми моментами. (Bazhayu vam yaskravoho novoho roku, napovnennogo velykymy peremohamy ta nezabutnymy momentamy.) - I wish you a vibrant New Year filled with great victories and unforgettable moments.

USEFUL UKRAINIAN WEATHER PHRASES

1. Ясно (Yasno) - Clear sky

2. Сонячно (Soniachno) - Sunny

3. Хмарно (Khmarno) - Cloudy

4. Похмурий день (Pokhmuryy den') - Overcast day

5. Туман (Tuman) - Fog

6. Дощ (Doshch) - Rain

7. Гроза (Groza) - Thunderstorm

8. Злива (Zlyva) - Downpour

9. Легкий дощ (Lehkyi doshch) - Light rain

10. Проливний дощ (Prolyvnyi doshch) - Heavy rain

11. Сніг (Snih) - Snow

12. Хуртовина (Khurtovyna) - Blizzard

13. Крижана дощова злива (Kryzhana doshchova zlyva) - Freezing rain

14. Град (Grad) - Hail

15. Льодяна крупа (L'yodyana krupa) - Sleet

16. Сильний вітер (Sylnyy viter) - Strong wind

17. Штиль (Shtyl') - Calm

18. Повітряна свіжість (Povitryana svizhist') - Fresh air

19. Тепло (Teplo) - Warm

20. Холодно (Kholodno) - Cold

21. Мороз (Moroz) - Frost

22. Падіння температури (Padinnya temperatury) - Temperature drop

23. Підйом температури (Pid'yom temperatury) - Temperature rise

24. Вологий (Volohyi) - Humid

25. Погожий (Pohozhyi) - Fair weather

26. Опади (Opadi) - Precipitation

27. Замерзання (Zamerzannya) - Freezing

28. Солов'їний спів (Solov'yinyy spiv) - Birds singing

29. Теплі вітри (Tepli vytry) - Warm winds

30. Зовсім холодно (Zovsim kholodno) - Very cold

31. Хуртовина зі снігом (Khurtovyna zi snihom) - Snowstorm

32. Льодовиковий вітер (L'yodovykovyy viter) - Glacier wind

33. Ожеледь (Ozheled') - Ice coating

34. Помірний дощ (Pomirnyy doshch) - Moderate rain

35. Торнадо (Tornado) - Tornado

Image by <a href="https://www.freepik.com/free-vector/hand-drawn-rainbow-design_7434972.htm?query=Rainbow">Freepik</a>

SPANISH

1. She visits her father.   Ella visita a su padre.
2. I call my friend.   Yo Telefono a mi amiga.
3. I have a lemon.   Yo tengo un limon.
4. I have a melon.   Yo tengo un melon.
   1. You take two oranges.

Vostros tomais dos naranjas.

6. I like tomatoes.   Me gustan los tomates.
7. I don't like beans   No me gustan las Judias
8. I don't like onions.

No me gustan las cebollas.

9. I drink   Yo bebo
8. You drink.   Tu bebes.
9. You drink juice.   Tu bebes Aqua.

10. They drink   Ellos beben.

11. They drink water and juice.

Ellos beben aqua y zumo.

12. You make tea.   Haces té.

13. I drink water with ice.   Yo bebo agua con hielo.

14. He would like black coffee.

El quisiera un cafe Americano.

15. She would like milk.   Ella quisiera leche.

16. I'm eating a sandwich.

Estoy comiendo un sándwich.

17. I'm eating a sandwich with cheese.

Estoy comiendo sándwich con queso.

18. I take a piece of bread.

Yo tomo un peddazo de pan.

19. We take two pieces of bread.

Nosotros tomamos dos trozos de queso.

20. Do you have fish?   ¿Tienes pescado?

21. Where is the salt?   ¿Dónde está la sal?

22. Can you bring me a fork?

¿Puedes traerme un tenedor?

23. Can you bring me a spoon?

¿Puedes traerme una cuchara?

24. Do you have a city map?   ¿Tienes un mapa de la ciudad?

25. Where is the post office?   ¿Dónde está la oficina de correos?

26. Where is the pharmacy?   ¿Dónde está la farmacia?

27. Where is the mall?   ¿Donde esta el centro comercial?

28. We need rice and bread.   Necesitamos arroz y pan.

29. We need tomatoes for the soup.   Necesitamos tomates para la sopa.

30. Where is the grocery store?   ¿Dónde esta el supermercado?

31. Where is the market? Dónde está el mercado?

32. Do you sell fruits and vegetables? Vosotros vendeis frutas y verduras?

33. We sell fruits and vegetables. Nosotros vendemos frutas y verduras.

34. I have to buy a book. Yo Tengo que comprar un libro.

35. I have to go to the bookstore. Yo Tengo que ir a la librería.

36. I have to go to the supermarket. Yo tengo que ir al supermercado.

USEFUL SPANISH PHRASES

- Hello. O-la
2. Adiós. (A-dee-os.) - Goodbye.
3. Por favor. ((Por-fa-bor.) - Please.
4. Gracias. (Gra-thi-as.) - Thank you.
5. De nada. (De na-da.) - You're welcome.
6. Sí. (See.) - Yes.
7. No. (No.) - No.
8. ¡Salud! (Sa-lud!) - Cheers!
9. Perdón. (Per-don.) - Excuse me.
10. ¿Cómo estás? (Co-mo es-tas?) - How are you?
11. Bien. (Bee-en.) - Fine/good.
12. Mal. (Mal.) - Bad.
13. Mucho gusto. (Mucho gus-to.) - Nice to meet you.
14. Lo siento. (Lo sien-to.) - I'm sorry.
15. ¿Dónde está el baño? (Don-de es-ta el ba-nio?) - Where is the bathroom?
16. ¿Cuánto cuesta? (Cuan-to cues-ta?) - How much does it cost?
17. ¿Habla inglés? (A-bla in-gles?) - Do you speak English?
18. No entiendo. (No en-tien-do.) - I don't understand.
19. ¿Puedo ayudarte? (Pwe-do a-yu-dar-te?) - Can I help you?
20. Estoy perdido. (Es-toy per-di-do.) - I am lost.

21. Me llamo... (Me lla-mo...) - My name is...

22. ¿Qué hora es? (Ke o-ra es?) - What time is it?

23. ¿Dónde puedo encontrar comida? (Don-de pwe-do en-contrar co-mi-da?) - Where can I find food?

24. Quisiera reservar una habitación. (Kee-sie-ra re-ser-var u-na ha-bi-ta-cion.) - I would like to book a room.

25. ¿Cómo se dice... en español? (Co-mo se dee-se... en es-pa-nyol?) - How do you say... in Spanish?

26. Estoy cansado/a. (Es-toy can-sa-do/a.) - I'm tired.

27. Estoy hambriento/a. (Es-toy am-brien-to/a.) - I'm hungry.

28. Estoy sediento/a. (Es-toy se-dien-to/a.) - I'm thirsty.

29. ¿Dónde puedo encontrar un taxi? (Don-de pwe-do en-contrar un ta-xi?) - Where can I find a taxi?

30. ¿Cuál es tu nombre? (Cwal es tu nombre?) - What is your name?

31. Nos vemos luego. (Nos ve-mos lwe-go.) - See you later.

32. Yo no sé. (Yo no se.) - I don't know.

33. ¿Cuál es la dirección? (Cwal es la di-rec-cion?) - What is the address?

34. ¿A qué hora es? (A ke o-ra es?) - What time is it?

35. Necesito ayuda. (Ne-ce-si-to a-yu-da.) - I need help.

36. ¡Feliz cumpleaños! (Fe-liz cump-le-a-nios!) - Happy birthday!

37. ¿Puedo pagar con tarjeta de crédito? (Pwe-do pa-gar kon tar-he-ta de kre-di-to?) - Can I pay with a credit card?

38. ¡Buen provecho! (Bwen pro-ve-cho!) - Enjoy your meal!

39. Tengo una pregunta. (Ten-go u-na pre-gonta.) - I have a question.

40. ¿Dónde puedo comprar souvenirs? (Don-de pwe-do kom-prar su-ve-nirs?) - Where can I buy souvenirs?

41. Disculpe. (Dis-kul-pe.) - Excuse me.

42. ¿Hablas más despacio, por favor? (A-blas mas des-pa-syo, por fa-bor?) - Can you speak more slowly, please?

43. ¿A qué hora abre/cierra? (A ke o-ra a-bre/sier-ra?) - What time does it open/close?

44. Está rico. (Es-ta ri-ko.) - It's delicious.

45. Ten cuidado. (Ten cwie-da-do.) - Be careful.

46. ¡Felicidades! (Fe-li-ci-da-des!) - Congratulations!

47. ¿Cuánto tiempo se tarda? (Cuan-to tjem-po se tar-da?) - How long does it take?

48. ¿Dónde puedo encontrar un cajero automático? (Don-de pwe-do en-contrar un ka-he-ro au-to-ma-ti-ko?) - Where can I find an ATM?

49. ¿Podría darme direcciones? (Pwo-dria dar-me di-rec-tions?) - Can you give me directions?

50. ¿Aceptan dólares? (A-sep-tan do-lares?) - Do you accept dollars?

51. Quiero comer algo. (Kye-ro ko-mer al-go.) - I want to eat something.

52. ¿A qué distancia está...? (A ke dis-tan-sya es-ta...?) - How far is...?

53. Está bien. (Es-ta byen.) - It's okay.

54. Tengo una reserva a nombre de... (Ten-go u-na re-ser-va a nob-re de...) - I have a reservation under the name of...

55. ¿Dónde puedo encontrar información turística? (Don-de pwe-do en-contrar in-for-ma-cion tu-ris-ti-ca?) - Where can I find tourist information?

56. ¿Cuál es el mejor restaurante aquí? (Cwal es el me-hor res-tau-ran-te a-ki?) - What is the best restaurant here?

57. ¿Me puedes recomendar algo para hacer? (Me pwe-des re-ko-men-dar al-go pa-ra ha-ser?) - Can you recommend something to do?

58. ¿Puedo tener la cuenta, por favor? (Pwe-do te-ner la kuen-ta, por fa-bor?) - Can I have the bill, please?

59. ¿Tienes cambio? (Tje-nes kam-bio?) - Do you have change?

60. ¿Dónde puedo cambiar dinero? (Don-de pwe-do kam-biar dje-ne-ro?) - Where can I exchange money?

61. ¿Dónde puedo encontrar un supermercado? (Don-de pwe-do en-contrar un su-per-mar-ka-do?) - Where can I find a supermarket?

62. ¡Qué bonito/a! (Ke bo-ni-to/a!) - How beautiful!

63. ¡Qué rico! (Ke ri-ko!) - How delicious!

64. ¡Hasta luego! (As-ta lwe-go!) - See you later!

65. ¿Cuánto tiempo queda? (Cuan-to tjem-po kwe-da?) - How much time is left?

66. ¿Me podría traer la carta? (Me po-dria tra-er la kar-ta?) - Could you bring me the menu?

67. ¿Me puedes ayudar con mi equipaje? (Me pwe-des a-yu-dar kon mi e-ki-pa-he?) - Can you help me with my luggage?

68. No importa. (No im-por-ta.) - It doesn't matter.

69. ¿Cuál es la estación de tren más cercana? (Cwal es la es-ta-cion de tren mas ser-ka-na?) - What is the nearest train station?

70. No comprendo. (No kom-pren-do.) - I don't understand.

71. ¿Cuál es tu comida típica? (Cwal es tu ko-mi-da tipi-ka?) - What is your typical food?

72. ¿Puedes repetir, por favor? (Pwe-des re-pe-tir, por fa-bor?) - Can you repeat that, please?

73. ¿Dónde puedo encontrar un banco? (Don-de pwe-do en-con-trar un ban-ko?) - Where can I find a bank?

74. ¿Puedes hablar más despacio? (Pwe-des a-blar mas des-pa-syo?) - Can you speak slower?

75. No tengo tiempo. (No ten-go tjem-po.) - I don't have time.

76. ¿Hay algún restaurante que recomiendes? (Ay al-gun res-tau-ran-te ke re-ko-myen-des?) - Is there any restaurant you recommend?

77. ¿Cuánto cuesta el billete/boleto? (Cua-to kues-ta el bi-je-te/bo-le-to?) - How much does the ticket cost?

78. ¡Qué interesante! (Ke in-te-re-san-te!) - How interesting!

79. ¿Dónde puedo encontrar un hospital? (Don-de pwe-do en-contrar un hos-pi-tal?) - Where can I find a hospital?

80. ¿Cuál es la mejor manera de llegar allí? (Cwal es la me-hor ma-ne-ra de lle-gar a-lly?) - What is the best way to get there?

81. ¿Puedes recomendarme un buen hotel? (Pwe-des re-ko-men-dar-me un bwien o-tel?) - Can you recommend a good hotel?

82. No tengo dinero. (No ten-go dje-ne-ro.) - I don't have money.

83. ¿Puedes explicarme esto? (Pwe-des eks-plee-kar-me es-to?) - Can you explain this to me?

84. ¿Hay Wi-Fi gratis aquí? (Ay Wi-Fi gra-tis a-ki?) - Is there free Wi-Fi here?

85. ¿Dónde puedo alquilar un coche/auto? (Don-de pwe-do al-ki-lar un ko-che/auto?) - Where can I rent a car?

86. ¿Cuánto tiempo se tarda en llegar allí? (Cuan-to tjem-po se tar-da en lle-gar a-lly?) - How long does it take to get there?

87. ¿Dónde puedo encontrar una farmacia? (Don-de pwe-do en-contrar u-na far-ma-sia?) - Where can I find a pharmacy?

88. ¿Qué recomiendas? (Ke re-ko-myen-das?) - What do you recommend?

89. ¿Me puedes dar un mapa? (Me pwe-des dar un ma-pa?) - Can you give me a map?

90. ¿Dónde puedo encontrar un buen restaurante? (Don-de pwe-do en-contrar un bwien res-tau-ran-te?) - Where can I find a good restaurant?

91. ¿Cuánto tiempo lleva? (Cuan-to tjem-po lle-va?) - How long does it take?

92. ¡Qué hermoso/a! (Ke er-mo-so/a!) - How beautiful!

93. ¿Puedo hablar con el encargado? (Pwe-do a-blar kon el en-kar-ga-do?) - Can I speak with the manager?

94. ¿Cuáles son los lugares turísticos más populares? (Cwales son los lu-ga-res tu-ris-ti-kos mas po-pu-la-res?) - What are the most popular tourist attractions?

95. ¿Cuándo abren/cierran? (Cwan-do a-bren/sier-ran?) - When do they open/close?

96. Quisiera una mesa para dos. (Kee-sie-ra u-na me-sa pa-ra dos.) -

USEFUL BUSINESS SPAINSIH PHRASES

1

1. Buenos días - Good morning (bweh-nos DEE-as)
2. Buenos días, ¿en qué puedo ayudarle? - Good morning, how can I assist you? (bweh-nos DEE-as, ehn keh pweh-do ah-yoo-DAR-leh)
3. ¿Cómo puedo ayudarlo? - How can I help you? (KOH-moh PWEH-do ah-yoo-DAR-loh)
4. Hola, ¿en qué puedo servirle? - Hello, how may I serve you? (OH-lah, ehn keh PWEH-do sehr-VEER-leh)
5. ¿En qué puedo colaborar? - How can I collaborate? (Ehn keh PWEH-do koh-lah-boh-RAR)
6. ¿Cuál es su nombre? - What is your name? (KWAHL es soo NOHM-bre)
7. Me llamo... - My name is... (Meh YAH-mo...)
8. Gusto en conocerte - Nice to meet you (GOOS-toh ehn koh-noh-SEHR-teh)
9. ¿En qué sector trabajas? - In which sector do you work? (Ehn keh SEK-tor trah-BAH-jas)
10. Trabajo en el sector financiero - I work in the financial sector (Trah-BAH-ho ehn el SEK-tor feen-ahn-SEE-ro)
11. ¿Cuál es tu empresa? - What is your company? (KWAHL es too em-PREH-sah)
12. Trabajo para... - I work for... (Trah-BAH-ho PAH-rah...)

13. ¿Podría tener su tarjeta de presentación? - Could I have your business card? (Poh-DREE-a TEH-ner soo tah-RREH-ta deh preh-sehn-tah-SEE-on)

14. Estoy interesado/a en su producto/servicio - I am interested in your product/service (Eh-STOY in-teh-reh-SAH-do/a ehn soo proh-DUK-toh/sehr-BEE-syo)

15. ¿Podrías enviarme más información al respecto? - Could you send me more information about it? (Poh-DREE-as en-vi-AHR-meh mahs een-fohr-mah-SEE-on ahl reh-SPEHK-toh)

16. Disculpe, ¿dónde se encuentra la sala de reuniones? - Excuse me, where can I find the meeting room? (Dees-KOOL-peh, DOHN-deh seh ehn-KWEN-tra lah SAH-lah deh reh-oo-KNEE-ones)

17. ¿A qué hora es nuestra reunión? - What time is our meeting? (AH keh O-rah es NOO-estrah reh-oo-KNEE-on)

18. La reunión está programada para las... - The meeting is scheduled for... (Lah reh-oo-KNEE-on es-TAH proh-gray-MAH-dah PAH-rah las...)

19. Necesitamos discutir los detalles del proyecto - We need to discuss the project details (Neh-seh-SEE-toh-mahs dee-skoo-TEER los deh-TAH-yes del proh-YEK-toh)

20. ¿Podríamos programar una conferencia telefónica? - Could we schedule a conference call? (Poh-DREE-ah-mos proh-gray-MAR oo-nah kon-feh-REN-see-ah teh-leh-FOH-nee-kah)

21. ¿Cuáles son los requisitos del trabajo? - What are the job requirements? (KWAH-les son los reh-kee-SEE-tohs del tra-BAH-ho)

22. Me gustaría solicitar una oferta de empleo - I would like to apply for a job offer (Me goos-ta-REE-a so-lee-see-TAR oo-na OFER-ta deh em-pleh-oh)

23. ¿Cuál es su política de devoluciones? - What is your return policy? (KWAHL es soo po-LEE-see-ah deh deh-voh-loo-see-OH-nes)

24. ¿Cuánto tiempo dura la garantía? - How long does the warranty last? (KWAHN-toh TYEM-po DOO-rah lah gah-ran-TEE-ah)

25. ¿Cuál es el precio por unidad? - What is the price per unit? (KWAHL es el PREH-see-oh por oo-NEE-dahd)

26. ¿Aceptan pagos con tarjeta de crédito? - Do you accept credit card payments? (Ah-SEP-tahn PAH-gos kon tah-RREH-tah deh KREH-dee-toh)

27. ¿Cuál es su política de envío? - What is your shipping policy? (KWAHL es soo po-LEE-see-ah deh en-BEE-oh)

28. ¿Cuál es la fecha límite? - What is the deadline? (KWAHL es lah FEH-cha LEE-me-teh)

29. Disculpe, necesito cancelar mi pedido - Excuse me, I need to cancel my order (Dees-KOOL-peh, neh-seh-SEE-toh kan-seh-LAR mee PEH-dee-doh)

30. ¿Cuál es su horario de atención al cliente? - What is your customer service schedule? (KWAHL es soo oh-RAH-ree-oh deh a-ten-SEE-on al klee-EN-teh)

31. ¿Podría hablar con el gerente? - Could I speak with the manager? (Poh-DREE-ah ah-BLAR kon el heh-REHN-teh)

32. Necesito hacer una reclamación - I need to make a complaint (Neh-seh-SEE-toh ah-SER oo-nah reh-kla-ma-SEE-on)

33. ¿Podría proporcionarme un presupuesto? - Could you provide me with a quote? (Poh-DREE-ah proh-vee-syo-NAR-meh oon preh-soo-PEH-sto)

34. Estoy muy satisfecho/a con el servicio recibido - I am very satisfied with the service I received (Eh-STOY moo-ee sah-tees-FEH-cho/a kon el sehr-BEE-syo reh-see-BEE-doh)

35. ¿Cuánto tiempo ha estado en el negocio? - How long have you been in business? (KWAHN-toh TYEM-po ah es-TAH-do en el neh-HO-see-yo)

36. ¿Cuál es su visión de futuro? - What is your vision for the future? (KWAHL es soo vee-SYON deh foo-TOO-roh)

37. Estamos buscando una asociación estratégica - We are looking for a strategic partnership (Es-TAH-mos boos-KAN-doh oo-nah a-so-see-ah-SEE-on es-trah-TEH-hee-kah)

38. ¿Cuál es su ventaja competitiva? - What is your competitive advantage? (KWAHL es soo ben-TA-ha kom-petee-TEE-bah)

39. ¿Cuánto cuesta el envío internacional? - How much is international shipping? (KWAHN-toh KWEHS-tah el en-BEE-oh een-ter-nah-see-o-NAHL)

USEFUL AIRPORT PHRASES IN SPANISH

1. ¡Hola! - Hello! (oh-lah)
2. Bienvenidos - Welcome (byen-veh-nee-dos)
3. ¿Cómo puedo ayudarte? - How can I help you? (koh-moh pweh-doh ah-yoo-dahr-teh)
4. ¿Dónde está la salida? - Where is the exit? (don-deh es-tah lah sah-lee-dah)
5. ¿Dónde está la puerta de embarque? - Where is the boarding gate? (don-deh es-tah lah pwer-tah deh em-bar-keh)
6. ¿Dónde puedo recoger mi equipaje? - Where can I pick up my luggage? (don-deh pweh-doh reh-koh-her mee eh-kee-pah-he)
7. Necesito ir a la terminal B - I need to go to terminal B (neh-seh-see-toh eer ah lah ter-mee-nal B)
8. ¿Dónde está la oficina de información? - Where is the information desk? (don-deh es-tah lah oh-fee-see-nah deh een-fohr-ma-see-on)
9. ¿A qué hora sale mi vuelo? - What time does my flight depart? (ah keh oh-rah sah-leh mee bwel-oh)
10. ¿Dónde puedo comprar un boleto? - Where can I buy a ticket? (don-deh pweh-doh kohm-prar oon boh-leh-toh)
11. ¿Dónde está el mostrador de facturación? - Where is the check-in counter? (don-deh es-tah el mohs-trah-dor deh fakh-too-ra-see-on)

12. ¿Tiene alguna oferta especial? - Do you have any special offers? (tee-eh-neh ahl-goo-nah oh-fehr-tah es-peh-see-al)

13. ¿Dónde están los baños? - Where are the restrooms? (don-deh es-tahn los bahn-yos)

14. ¿Dónde puedo cambiar dinero? - Where can I exchange money? (don-deh pweh-doh kahm-bee-ahr dee-neh-ro)

15. ¿Hay wifi disponible en el aeropuerto? - Is there wifi available at the airport? (ay wee-fee ah-vee-lah-bleh en el ay-eh-ro-pwer-toh)

16. ¿Dónde se recogen los taxis? - Where do you pick up taxis? (don-deh seh reh-koh-hehn los tah-xees)

17. ¿Dónde puedo obtener un carrito para el equipaje? - Where can I get a cart for the luggage? (don-deh pweh-doh ohb-teh-nehr oon kah-ree-toh pah-rah el eh-kee-pah-he)

18. ¿Cuál es el número de vuelo? - What is the flight number? (kwal es el noo-meh-ro deh bwel-oh)

19. ¿Dónde está la zona de espera? - Where is the waiting area? (don-deh es-tah lah soh-nah deh es-peh-rah)

20. ¿Hay algún restaurante cerca? - Is there a restaurant nearby? (ay ahl-goon res-tow-rahn-te ser-kah)

21. ¿Cuál es el límite de peso para el equipaje? - What is the weight limit for the luggage? (kwal es el lee-mee-teh deh peh-soh pah-rah el eh-kee-pah-he)

22. ¿Dónde puedo encontrar un mapa del aeropuerto? - Where can I find an airport map? (don-deh pweh-doh en-kon-trar oon mah-pah del ay-eh-ro-pwer-toh)

23. ¿Hay algún cajero automático en el aeropuerto? - Is there an ATM at the airport? (ay ahl-goon kah-heh-roh ah-toh-mah-tee-coh en el ay-eh-ro-pwer-toh)

24. ¿Dónde puedo hacer el check-in? - Where can I check in? (don-deh pweh-doh ah-sehr el chehk-een)

25. ¿Cuál es la hora de llegada? - What is the arrival time? (kwal es lah oh-rah deh yeh-gah-dah)

26. ¿Dónde puedo encontrarte? - Where can I meet you? (don-deh pweh-doh en-kon-trahr-teh)

27. ¿Dónde puedo encontrar un carrito de equipajes? - Where can I find a luggage cart? (don-deh pweh-doh en-kon-trahr oon kah-ree-toh deh eh-kee-pah-hes)

28. ¿Hay algún vuelo retrasado? - Is there any delayed flight? (ay ahl-goon bwel-oh reh-trah-sah-doh)

29. ¿Dónde puedo hacer una reservación de hotel? - Where can I make a hotel reservation? (don-deh pweh-doh ah-sehr oo-nah reh-sehr-vah-see-on deh o-tehl)

30. ¿Dónde puedo encontrar una taquilla automática? - Where can I find a self-service ticket machine? (don-deh pweh-doh en-kon-trahr oo-nah tah-kee-yah ah-toh-mah-tee-cah)

31. ¿Cuál es el horario de vuelos internacionales? - What is the schedule for international flights? (kwal es el oh-rah-ree-oh deh bwel-ohs een-ter-nah-see-oh-nah-lehs)

32. ¿Dónde puedo obtener un carnet de embarque? - Where can I get a boarding pass? (don-deh pweh-doh ohb-teh-nehr oon kahr-neh deh em-bar-keh)

33. ¿Hay un mostrador de servicio al cliente? - Is there a customer service counter? (hay oon mohs-trah-dor deh sehr-vee-syo al klee-en-teh)

34. ¿Dónde puedo encontrar un enchufe para cargar mi teléfono? - Where can I find a plug to charge my phone? (don-deh pweh-doh en-kon-trahr oon en-choo-feh pah-rah kahr-gahr mee teh-leh-foh-noh)

35. ¿Hay algún vuelo directo a esta ciudad? - Is there any direct flight to this city? (ay ahl-goon bwel-oh dee-rehk-toh ah eh-stah seeh-dad)

MULTILINGUAL PHRASE BOOK 125

36. ¿Podría darme un folleto de información turística? - Could you give me a tourist information brochure? (po-dree-ah dahr-meh oon fol-leh-toh deh een-fohr-ma-see-on too-ree-stee-kah)

37. ¿Dónde puedo encontrar una farmacia? - Where can I find a pharmacy? (don-deh pweh-doh en-kon-trahr oo-nah fahr-mah-see-ah)

38. ¿Cuál es el número de la puerta de embarque? - What is the gate number? (kwal es el noo-meh-ro deh lah pwer-tah deh em-bar-keh)

39. ¿Dónde puedo encontrar la sala de espera VIP? - Where can I find the VIP waiting lounge? (don-deh pweh-doh en-kon-trahr lah sah-lah deh es-peh-rah VIP)

40. ¿Podría ayudarme con mi equipaje? - Could you help me with my luggage? (po-dree-ah ah-yoo-dar-meh kon mee eh-kee-pah-he)

41. ¿Dónde puedo encontrar la recogida de equipajes? - Where can I find the baggage claim? (don-deh pweh-doh en-kon-trahr lah reh-koh-hee-dah deh eh-kee-pah-hes)

42. ¿Cuánto tiempo dura el vuelo? - How long does the flight last? (kwahn-toh tee-em-poh doo-rah el bwel-oh)

43. ¿Dónde puedo comprar comida para llevar? - Where can I buy takeaway food? (don-deh pweh-doh kohm-prar koh-mee-dah pah-rah lley-var)

44. ¿Hay un área de fumadores? - Is there a smoking area? (hay oon ah-reh-ah deh foo-mah-doh-res)

45. ¿Dónde puedo encontrar una máquina expendedora de billetes? - Where can I find a ticket vending machine? (don-deh pweh-doh en-kon-trahr oo-nah mah-kee-nah ex-pen-deh-doh-rah deh bee-yeh-tes)

46. ¿Cuál es la zona de reclamo de equipajes? - What is the baggage claim area? (kwal es lah soh-nah deh reh-klah-mo deh eh-kee-pah-hes)

47. ¿Dónde puedo encontrar un servicio de transporte al hotel? - Where can I find a hotel transportation service? (don-deh pweh-doh en-kon-trahr oon sehr-vee-syo deh trans-por-teh al o-tehl)

48. ¿Dónde está la salida de emergencia? - Where is the emergency exit? (don-deh es-tah lah sah-lee-dah deh eh-mehr-hen-see-ah

49. ¿Cuál es el horario de la última llamada? - What is the schedule for the final boarding call? (kwal es el oh-rah-ree-oh deh lah ool-tee-mah yah-mah-dah)

50. ¿Dónde puedo reclamar un objeto perdido? - Where can I claim a lost item? (don-deh pweh-doh reh-kla-mar oon ohb-hek-toh per-dee-doh)

Numbers in Spanish

1 - uno (ooh-no)
2 - dos (dohs)
3 - tres (trehs)
4 - cuatro (kwah-troh)
5 - cinco (seeng-koh)
6 - seis (sehs)
7 - siete (see-eh-teh)
8 - ocho (oh-choh)
9 - nueve (nweh-veh)
10 - diez (dyehs)
11 - once (ohn-seh)
12 - doce (doh-seh)
13 - trece (treh-seh)
14 - catorce (kah-tohr-seh)
15 - quince (keen-seh)
16 - dieciséis (dyeh-see-sehs)
17 - diecisiete (dyeh-see-syeh-teh)
18 - dieciocho (dyeh-see-oh-choh)
19 - diecinueve (dyeh-see-nweh-veh)
20 - veinte (veh-een-teh)
21 - veintiuno (veh-een-tee-oo-noh)

22 - veintidós (veh-een-tee-dohs)

23 - veintitrés (veh-een-tee-trehs)

24 - veinticuatro (veh-een-tee-kwah-troh)

25 - veinticinco (veh-een-tee-seeng-koh)

26 - veintiséis (veh-een-tee-sehs)

27 - veintisiete (veh-een-tee-see-eh-teh)

28 - veintiocho (veh-een-tee-oh-choh)

29 - veintinueve (veh-een-tee-nweh-veh)

30 - treinta (treh-een-tah)

40 - cuarenta (kwah-rehn-tah)

50 - cincuenta (seen-kwehn-tah)

60 - sesenta (seh-sehn-tah)

70 - setenta (seh-tehn-tah)

80 - ochenta (oh-chehn-tah)

90 - noventa (noh-vehn-tah)

100 - cien (syehn)

USEFUL HOLIDAY SPANISH PHRASES

1. ¡Felices fiestas! - Happy holidays! (feh-lee-sehs fee-ehs-tahs)

2. Navidad - Christmas (nah-bee-dahd)

3. Año Nuevo - New Year (ah-nyoh nweh-boh)

4. ¡Feliz Navidad! - Merry Christmas! (feh-lees nah-bee-dahd)

5. Prospero Año Nuevo - Happy New Year! (prohs-peh-roh ah-nyoh nweh-boh)

6. Nochebuena - Christmas Eve (noh-cheh-bweh-nah)

7. Día de Acción de Gracias - Thanksgiving (dee-ah deh ahk-see-on deh grah-see-ahs)

8. Regalos - Gifts (reh-gah-lohs)

9. Cena de Navidad - Christmas dinner (seh-nah deh nah-bee-dahd)

10. Reyes Magos - Three Wise Men (reh-yes mah-gohs)

11. Brindis - Toast (breendees)

12. Villancicos - Christmas carols (bee-yahn-kee-kohs)

13. Luces - Lights (loo-sehs)

14. Tradiciones - Traditions (trah-dee-see-oh-nehs)

15. Árbol de Navidad - Christmas tree (ahr-bohl deh nah-bee-dahd)

16. Felicitaciones - Greetings (feh-lee-see-tah-see-oh-nehs)

17. Adornos navideños - Christmas decorations (ah-dor-nohs nah-vee-deh-nyohs)

18. Paz en la Tierra - Peace on Earth (pahs en la tyehr-rah)

19. Nochevieja - New Year's Eve (noh-cheh-vyeh-hah)

20. Deseos de Navidad - Christmas wishes (deh-seh-ohs deh nah-bee-dahd)

21. Guirnaldas - Garlands (gee-ernahl-dahs)

22. Espíritu navideño - Christmas spirit (eh-spee-ree-too nah-vee-deh-nyoh)

23. Festejos - Celebrations (fehs-teh-hohs)

24. Canciones navideñas - Christmas songs (kahn-see-oh-nehs nah-vee-deh-nyahs)

25. Agradecimiento - Gratitude (ah-grah-deh-see-mee-ehn-toh)

26. Feliz día festivo - Happy holiday (feh-lees dee-ah fehs-tee-boh)

27. Tradición familiar - Family tradition (trah-dee-see-yohn fah-mee-lee-yahr)

28. Comida navideña - Christmas food (koh-mee-dah nah-vee-deh-nyah)

29. Feliz año nuevo - Happy New Year (feh-lees ah-nyoh nweh-boh)

30. Fiesta de Nochevieja - New Year's Eve Party (fee-es-tah deh noh-cheh-vyeh-hah)

31. Bendiciones - Blessings (behn-dee-see-oh-nehs)

32. Salsa música de Navidad - Christmas music playlist (sahl-sah moo-see-kah deh nah-bee-dahd)

33. Espumillón - Tinsel (ehs-poo-mee-yohn)

34. Tarjetas de felicitación - Greeting cards (tahr-heh-tahs deh feh-lee-see-tah-see-ohn)

35. Santa Claus - Santa Claus (sahn-tah klowhs)

36. Alegría - Joy (ah-leh-gree-ah)

37. Compartir - Share (kohm-pahr-teer)

38. Serenatas - Serenades (seh-reh-nahtahs)

39. Estrella de Navidad - Christmas star (ehs-treh-yah deh nah-bee-dahd)

40. Brilla, brilla pequeña estrella - Twinkle, twinkle little star (bree-yah, bree-yah peh-keh-nyah ehs-treh-yah)

USEFUL TELEPHONE PHRASES IN SPANISH

. ¡Hola! - Hello! (oh-lah)

2. ¿Está Juan? - Is Juan there? (ehs-tah hwahn)

3. ¿Puede dejarme un mensaje? - Can you leave me a message? (pweh-deh deh-hahr-meh oon meh-sah-heh)

4. ¿Podría hablar con el gerente, por favor? - Could I speak with the manager, please? (poh-dree-ah ah-blahr kohn ehl heh-rehn-teh, pohr fah-bor)

5. ¿Cuál es tu número de teléfono? - What is your phone number? (kwahl ehs too noo-meh-roh deh teh-leh-foh-noh)

6. ¿Puede comunicarme con el departamento de ventas? - Can you connect me to the sales department? (pweh-deh koh-moo-nee-kahr-meh kohn ehl deh-pahr-tah-mehn-toh deh behn-tahs)

7. No puedo escuchar bien, ¿puede hablar más despacio? - I can't hear well, can you speak slower? (noh pweh-doh ehs-koo-char byehn, pweh-deh ah-blahr mahs dehs-pah-see-oh)

8. ¿Quién habla? - Who is speaking? (kyehn ah-blah)

9. Lo siento, llamaste al número equivocado. - I'm sorry, you've reached the wrong number. (loh syehn-toh, yah-mahs-teh ahl noo-meh-roh eh-kee-boh-kah-doh)

10. ¿Puedo tomar un mensaje? - Can I take a message? (pweh-doh toh-mahr oon meh-sah-heh)

(Continued in the next line)

11. Perdí tu número, ¿me lo puedes repetir? - I lost your number, can you repeat it? (pehr-dee too noo-meh-roh, meh loh pweh-dehs reh-peh-teer)

12. ¿A qué hora puedo devolverte la llamada? - What time can I call you back? (ah keh oh-rah pweh-doh deh-vohl-vehr-teh lah yah-mah-dah)

13. ¿Cuánto cuesta la llamada? - How much does the call cost? (kwahn-toh kwehs-tah lah yah-mah-dah)

14. ¿Hay alguna oferta o promoción disponible? - Is there any offer or promotion available? (eye ahl-goo-nah oh-fehr-tah oh pro-moh-see-on ahb-yah-leh)

15. ¿Está ocupado/a el/la línea? - Is the line busy? (ehs-tah oh-koo-pah-doh/ah ehl/lah lee-nyah)

16. ¿Puedo hablar con el departamento de servicio al cliente? - Can I speak with the customer service department? (pweh-doh ah-blahr kohn ehl deh-pahr-tah-mehn-toh deh sehr-vee-syoh ahl klee-ehn-teh)

17. ¿Puedes repetir eso, por favor? - Can you repeat that, please? (pweh-dehs reh-peh-teer eh-so, pohr fah-bor)

18. ¿Me puedes poner en espera un momento? - Can you put me on hold for a moment? (meh pweh-dehs poh-nehr ehn ehs-peh-rah oon moh-mehn-toh)

19. ¿Quién es tu proveedor de servicios telefónicos? - Who is your telephone service provider? (kyehn ehs too proh-veh-dohr deh sehr-vee-syohs teh-leh-foh-neekos)

20. ¿De parte de quién? - Who is calling? (deh pahr-teh deh kyehn) (Continued in the next line)

21. Una llamada internacional - An international call (oo-nah yah-mah-dah een-tehr-nah-see-oh-nahl)

22. ¿Puedo dejar un recado? - Can I leave a message? (pweh-doh deh-hahr oon reh-kah-doh)

23. ¿Cuánto tiempo va a durar la llamada? - How long will the call last? (kwahn-toh tee-ehm-poh bah ah doo-rahr lah yah-mah-dah)

24. ¿Dónde puedo encontrar una cabina telefónica? - Where can I find a telephone booth? (dohn-deh pweh-doh ehn-kohn-trahr oo-nah kah-bee-nah teh-leh-foh-nee-kah)

25. ¿Cuál es el prefijo telefónico de este país? - What is the telephone dialing code for this country? (kwahl ehs ehl preh-fee-ho teh-leh-foh-nee-koh deh ehs-teh pah-ees)

26. ¿Está disponible el servicio de contestador automático? - Is the voicemail service available? (ehs-tah ahb-yah-leh ehl sehr-vee-syoh deh kohn-tehs-tah-dohr au-toh-mah-tee-koh)

27. ¿Qué número de extensión tengo que marcar? - What extension number do I need to dial? (keh noo-meh-roh deh ehks-tehn-see-on tohn-goh keh mahr-kahr)

28. ¿Puede llamar más tarde? - Can you call back later? (pweh-deh yah-mahr mahs tar-deh)

29. ¿Hay cobertura telefónica en esta zona? - Is there phone coverage in this area? (eye koh-behr-too-rah teh-leh-foh-nee-kah ehn ehs-tah soh-nah)

30. ¿Podría hablar con la persona encargada? - Could I speak with the person in charge? (poh-dree-ah ah-blahr kohn lah pehr-soh-nah ehn-kahr-gah-dah)

(Continued in the next line)

31. ¿Hay un teléfono público cerca de aquí? - Is there a public telephone nearby? (eye oon teh-leh-foh-noh poh-blee-koh sehr-kah deh ah-kee)

32. ¿Puede recomendar algún plan telefónico? - Can you recommend any phone plan? (pweh-deh reh-koh-mehn-dahr ahl-goon plahn teh-leh-foh-nee-koh)

33. ¿La llamada es gratuita? - Is the call free of charge? (lah yah-mah-dah ehs groo-ee-tah)

34. ¿Me podría transferir a otra extensión? - Could you transfer me to another extension? (meh poh-dree-ah trahn-feh-reer ah oh-trah ehks-tehn-see-on)

35. ¿Hay un problema con mi línea telefónica? - Is there a problem with my phone line? (eye oon proh-bleh-mah kohn mee lee-nyah teh-leh-foh-nee-kah)

36. ¿Puedo hacer una llamada a cobro revertido? - Can I make a collect call? (pweh-doh ah-sehr oo-nah yah-mah-dah ah koh-broh reh-vehr-tee-doh)

37. ¿Cuántos minutos me quedan? - How many minutes do I have left? (kwahn-tohs mee-noo-tohs meh keh-dahn)

USEFUL POSTAL PHRASES IN SPANISH

Hola, ¿en qué puedo ayudarte? - Hello, how can I help you? (oh-lah, ehn keh pweh-doh ah-yoo-dahr-teh)

2. Quisiera enviar esta carta. - I would like to send this letter. (kee-see-eh-rah ehn-vee-ahr eh-stah kahr-tah)

3. ¿Cuánto cuesta enviar un paquete a otro país? - How much does it cost to send a package to another country? (kwahn-toh kwehs-tah ehn-vee-ahr oon pah-keh-teh ah oh-troh pah-ees)

4. Necesito comprar sellos. - I need to buy stamps. (neh-seh-see-toh kohm-prahr seh-yohs)

5. ¿Adónde puedo enviar un paquete certificado? - Where can I send a certified package? (ah-dohn-deh pweh-doh ehn-vee-ahr oon pah-keh-teh sehr-tee-fee-kah-doh)

6. ¿Tienes sobres disponibles? - Do you have envelopes available? (tee-eh-nehs soh-brehs ahb-yah-lehs)

7. Quiero hacer una transferencia de dinero. - I want to make a money transfer. (kee-eh-roh ah-sehr oo-nah trahn-feh-rehn-see-ah deh dee-neh-roh)

8. ¿Cuál es el horario de atención al cliente? - What is the customer service opening hours? (kwahl ehs ehl oh-rah-ree-oh deh ah-tehn-see-on ahl klee-ehn-teh)

9. ¿Puedo comprar una tarjeta telefónica aquí? - Can I buy a phone card here? (pweh-doh kohm-prahr oo-nah tahr-heh-tah teh-leh-foh-nee-kah ah-kee)

10. ¿Dónde está la oficina de correos más cercana? - Where is the nearest post office? (dohn-deh ehs-tah lah oh-fee-see-nah deh koh-rreh-os mahs sehr-kah-nah)

(Continued in the next line)

11. Quiero enviar una carta certificada. - I want to send a certified letter. (kee-eh-roh ehn-vee-ahr oo-nah kahr-tah sehr-tee-fee-kah-dah)

12. ¿Puedo llenar el formulario aquí? - Can I fill out the form here? (pweh-doh yeh-nahr ehl for-moo-lah ah-kee)

13. Necesito enviar un paquete urgente. - I need to send an urgent package. (neh-seh-see-toh ehn-vee-ahr oon pah-keh-teh oor-hehn-teh)

14. ¿Hay un buzón de correo cerca de aquí? - Is there a mailbox nearby? (eye oon boo-sohn deh koh-rreh oohn-kee-ah-kee)

15. Quiero pedir un duplicado de mi comprobante de envío. - I want to request a duplicate of my shipping receipt. (kee-eh-roh peh-deer oon doo-plee-kah-doh deh mee kohm-proh-bahn-teh deh ehn-vee-oh)

16. ¿Aceptan pagos con tarjeta de crédito? - Do you accept credit card payments? (ah-sehp-tahn pah-gohs kohn tahra-heh-tah deh kreh-dee-toh)

17. ¿Cuándo llegará mi paquete? - When will my package arrive? (kwahn-doh yeh-gah-rah mee pah-keh-teh)

18. Quisiera enviar este sobre por correo aéreo. - I would like to send this envelope by airmail. (kee-see-eh-rah ehn-vee-ahr eh-steh soh-breh pohr koh-rreh-o ah-eh-reh-oh)

19. ¿Puedo obtener un número de seguimiento? - Can I get a tracking number? (pweh-doh ohb-teh-nehr oon noo-meh-roh deh seh-goo-ee-mee-ehn-toh)

20. ¿Hay un límite de peso para los envíos? - Is there a weight limit for shipments? (eye oon lee-meh-teh deh peh-soh pah-rah lohs ehn-vee-ohs)

(Continued in the next line)

21. Quiero cambiar la dirección de destino. - I want to change the destination address. (kee-eh-roh kahm-bee-ahr lah dee-rehk-see-on deh dee-nehs-toh)

22. ¿Cuál es el plazo de entrega estimado? - What is the estimated delivery time? (kwahl ehs ehl plah-soh deh en-treh-gah es-tee-mah-doh)

23. ¿Dónde puedo reclamar un paquete perdido? - Where can I claim a lost package? (dohn-deh pweh-doh reh-klah-mahr oon pah-keh-teh sehr-dee-doh)

24. Quisiera enviar este paquete como correo certificado. - I would like to send this package as certified mail. (kee-see-eh-rah ehn-vee-ahr eh-steh pah-keh-teh koh-moh koh-rreh-oh sehr-tee-fee-kah-doh)

25. ¿Puedes ayudarme a completar el formulario? - Can you help me fill out the form? (pweh-dehs ah-yoo-dahr-meh ah kohm-pleh-tahr ehl for-moo-lah)

26. ¿Dónde puedo obtener sellos internacionales? - Where can I get international stamps? (dohn-deh pweh-doh ohb-teh-nehr seh-yohs een-tehr-nah-syoh-nah-lehs)

27. Necesito enviar un paquete frágil. - I need to send a fragile package. (neh-seh-see-toh ehn-vee-ahr oon pah-keh-teh frah-heel)

28. ¿Hay algún seguro para los envíos? - Is there any insurance for shipments? (eye ahl-goon seu-roh pah-rah lohs ehn-vee-ohs)

29. Me gustaría recibir las notificaciones por correo electrónico. - I would like to receive notifications via email. (meh goos-tah-ree-ah reh-see-beer lahs noh-tee-fee-kah-see-ohnes pohr koh-rreh-oh eh-lehk-troh-nee-koh)

30. ¿Hay restricciones sobre los artículos enviados? - Are there restrictions on the items being sent? (eye rehs-treek-see-oh-nes soh-breh lohs ahr-tee-koo-lohs ehn-vee-ah-dos)

(Continued in the next line)

31. ¿Cuál es la tarifa de envío para este paquete? - What is the shipping fee for this package? (kwahl ehs lah tah-ree-fah deh ehn-vee-oh pah-rah ehs-teh pah-keh-teh)

32. Quisiera solicitar un cambio de dirección de entrega. - I would like to request a change of delivery address. (kee-see-eh-rah soh-lee-see-tahr oon kahm-bee-oh deh dee-rehk-see-on deh en-treh-gah)

33. ¿Tienen servicios de embalaje disponibles? - Do you have packing services available? (tyeh-nehn sehr-vee-syohs deh ehm-bah-lah-heh ahb-yah-lehs)

34. ¿En cuánto tiempo llega a su destino un envío nacional? - How long does it take for a domestic shipment to reach its destination? (ehn kwahn-toh tee-ehm-poh yeh-gah ah soo dee-nehs-toh oon ehn-vee-oh nah-syoh-nahl)

35. Quiero enviar una tarjeta de felicitación. - I want to send a greeting card. (kee-eh-roh ehn-vee-ahr oo-nah tahrr-heh-tah deh feh-lee-see-tah-see-on)

36. ¿Puedo obtener una copia del comprobante de envío? - Can I get a copy of the shipping receipt? (pweh-doh ohb-teh-nehr oo-nah koh-pee-ah del kohm-proh-bahn-teh deh ehn-vee-oh)

37. ¿Dónde puedo comprar sobres prepagados? - Where can I buy prepaid envelopes? (dohn-deh pweh-doh kohm-prahr soh-brehss preh-pah-gah-dohs)

38. Quiero enviar un paquete con seguro. - I want to send a package with insurance

USEFUL WEATHER PHRASES IN SPANISH

1. Hace sol. - It's sunny. (ah-seh sohl)
2. Hace calor. - It's hot. (ah-seh kah-lor)
3. Hace frío. - It's cold. (ah-seh free-oh)
4. Está nublado. - It's cloudy. (ehs-tah noo-blah-doh)
5. Está nevando. - It's snowing. (ehs-tah neh-vahn-doh)
6. Hay viento. - It's windy. (eye vee-ehn-toh)
7. Hay niebla. - It's foggy. (eye nee-eh-blah)
8. Está lloviendo. - It's raining. (ehs-tah yoh-vee-ehn-doh)
9. El cielo está despejado. - The sky is clear. (ehl see-eh-loh ehs-tah dehs-peh-hah-doh)
10. Hay tormenta. - There's a storm. (eye tor-mehn-tah)
11. Hace buen tiempo. - The weather is good. (ah-seh bwehn tee-ehm-poh)
12. Hace mal tiempo. - The weather is bad. (ah-seh mahl tee-ehm-poh)
13. Hace fresco. - It's cool. (ah-seh fres-koh)
14. Está húmedo. - It's humid. (ehs-tah oo-meh-doh)
15. Hay un arcoíris. - There's a rainbow. (eye oon ahr-koh-ee-rees)
16. Está soleado. - It's sunny. (ehs-tah soh-leh-ah-doh)
17. Hay una brisa suave. - There's a gentle breeze. (eye oo-nah bree-sah swah-veh)

18. Está agradable. - It's pleasant. (ehs-tah ah-gray-dah-bleh)

19. Hay fuertes ráfagas de viento. - There are strong gusts of wind. (eye foo-ehr-tehs rah-fah-gahs deh vee-ehn-toh)

20. Hay un clima cambiante. - The weather is changeable. (eye oon klee-mah kahm-bee-ahn-teh)

21. Está helado. - It's freezing. (ehs-tah eh-lah-doh)

22. Hay chubascos. - There are showers. (eye choo-bahs-kohs)

23. Hay granizo. - There's hail. (eye grah-nee-soh)

24. Hay una bruma ligera. - There's a light mist. (eye oo-nah broo-mah lee-eh-rah)

25. Hace mucho viento. - It's very windy. (ah-seh moo-choh vee-ehn-toh)

26. Hay relámpagos. - There are lightning strikes. (eye reh-lahm-pah-gohs)

27. Hay truenos. - There's thunder. (eye trweh-nohs)

28. Está despejado y seco. - It's clear and dry. (ehs-tah dehs-peh-hah-doh ee seh-koh)

29. Hay una ráfaga de calor. - There's a heatwave. (eye oo-nah rah-fah-gah deh kah-lor)

30. Hay un frente frío. - There's a cold front. (eye oon frehn-teh free-oh)

31. El clima está inestable. - The weather is unstable. (ehl klee-mah ehs-tah ee-nehs-tah-bleh)

32. Hace bochorno. - It's muggy. (ah-seh boh-chor-noh)

33. Hay rocío. - There's dew. (eye roh-see-oh)

34. Hay una ola de calor. - There's a heatwave. (eye oo-nah oh-lah deh kah-lor)

35. Hace viento fresco. - It's breezy. (ah-seh vee-ehn-toh fres-koh)

36. Está parcialmente nublado. - It's partly cloudy. (ehs-tah pahr-see-ahl-mehn-teh noo-blah-doh)

37. Hay una tormenta eléctrica. - There's a thunderstorm. (eye oo-nah tor-mehn-tah eh-lehk-tree-kah)

38. Hace mucho frío. - It's very cold. (ah-seh moo-choh free-oh)

39. Está despejado con algunas nubes. - It's clear with some clouds. (ehs-tah dehs-peh-hah-doh kohn ahl-goo-nahs noo-bes)

40. Hay llovizna. - There's drizzle. (eye yoh-vee-znah)

41. Hace buen clima. - The weather is nice. (ah-seh bwehn klee-mah)

42. Está fresco y agradable. - It's cool and pleasant. (ehs-tah fres-koh ee ah-gray-dah-bleh)

43. Hay un frente cálido. - There's a warm front. (eye oon frehn-teh kahl-ee-doh)

44. Hace mucho calor. - It's very hot. (ah-seh moo-choh kah-lor)

45. Hay una cortina de lluvia. - There's a curtain of rain. (eye oo-nah kor-tee-nah deh yoh-vee-ah)

46. Hace buen tiempo para salir. - It's good weather to go out. (ah-seh bwehn tee-ehm-poh pah-rah sah-leer)

47. Está despejado y soleado. - It's clear and sunny. (ehs-tah dehs-peh-hah-doh ee soh-leh-ah-doh)

48. Hace un clima agradable y seco. - It's a pleasant and dry climate. (ah-seh oon klee-mah ah-gray-dah-bleh ee seh-koh)

49. Hay un frente de tormenta. - There's a storm front. (eye oon frehn-teh deh tor-mehn-tah)

50. Hace buen tiempo para hacer actividades al aire libre. - It's good weather to do outdoor activities. (ah-seh bwehn tee-ehm-poh pah-rah ah-sehr ahk-tee-vee-dah-dehs ahl ah-ee-reh lee-breh)

I

Image by <a href="https://www.freepik.com/free-photo/rainbow-sky-with-view-city_34136945.htm">Freepik</a>

GERMAN

1. She visits her father.

Sie besucht ihren Vater.

2. I telephone my friend.   I

Ich rufe meinen Freund an

3. I travel a lot.

Ich reise viel.

4. I have a lemon.

Ich habe eine Zitrone.

5. I have a melon.

Ich habe eine Melone.

6. You take two oranges Du nimmst zwei Orangen

7. I like tomatoes.

Ich mag Tomaten.

8. I don't like beans.

Ich mag keine Bohnen.

9. I don't like onions.

Ich mag keine Zwiebeln.

10. I drink.

Ich trinke.

11. I drink juice.

Ich trinke Saft.

12. You drink
Du trinkst.

13. You drink water   Du trinkst Wasser.

14. They drink water and juice.
Sie trinken Wasser und Saft.

15. You make tea.   Du machst Tee.

16. I drink water with ice.   Ich trinke Wasser mit Eis.

17. He would like black ice.
Er möchte schwarzen Kaffee.

18. She would like milk.   Sie möchte Milch.

19. I'm eating a sandwich.   Ich esse ein Sandwich.

20. I'm eating a sandwich with cheese.
Ich esse Sandwich mit Käse.

21. I take a piece of bread.
Ich nehme ein Stück Brot.

22. We take two pieces of cheese.
Wir nehmen zwei Stück Käse.

23. Do you have fish?   Haben sie Fisch?

24. Where is the salt? Wo ist das Salz?

25. Can you bring me a fork?
Kannst du mir eine Gabel bringen?

26. Can you bring me a spoon?
Kannst du mir einen Löffel bringen?

27. Do you have a city map?   Haben Sie einen Stadtplan?

28. Where is the post office?   Wo ist die Post?

29. Where is the pharmacy?   Wo ist die Apotheke?

30. Where is the mall?   Wo ist das Einkaufszentrum?

31. We need rice and bread.   Wir brauchen Reis und Brot.

32. We need tomatoes for the soup. Wir brauchen Tomaten für die Suppe.

33. Where is the grocery store?   Wo ist der Supermarkt?

34. Where is the market?   Wo ist der Markt?

35. Do you sell fruits and vegetables?   Verkaufen Sie Obst und Gemüse?

36. We sell fruits and vegetables.   Wir verkaufen Obst und Gemüse.

37. I have to buy a book.   Ich muss ein Buch kaufen.

38. I have to go to the book store.   Ich muss in den Buchladen.

39. I have to go to the supermarket.   Ich muss zum Supermarkt.

USEFUL GERMAN PHRASES

1. Guten Morgen. - Good morning. (goo-ten mor-gen)

2. Auf Wiedersehen. - Goodbye. (auf vee-der-zey-en)

3. Danke schön. - Thank you very much. (dahn-kuh shern)

4. Wie geht es Ihnen? - How are you? (vee geht es ee-nen)

5. Ja - Yes. (yah)

6. Nein - No. (nine)

7. Entschuldigung. - Excuse me. (ent-shool-di-gung)

8. Ich verstehe nicht. - I don't understand. (ikh fair-steh-eh nikht)

9. Bitte. - Please. (bit-teh)

10. Es tut mir leid. - I'm sorry. (es toot meer lite)

11. Wie heißt du? - What's your name? (vee hyst doo)

12. Woher kommst du? - Where are you from? (vor-hair komst doo)

13. Ich spreche kein Deutsch. - I don't speak German. (ikh sh-preh-khe kine doytsh)

14. Ich brauche Hilfe. - I need help. (ikh brow-khe hil-feh)

15. Einen Moment bitte. - One moment please. (ay-nen mo-men bit-teh)

16. Wie spät ist es? - What time is it? (vee shpayt ist es)

17. Wo ist die Toilette? - Where is the restroom? (vo ist dee toa-let-teh)

18. Gute Nacht. - Goodnight. (goo-teh naht)

19. Wie alt bist du? - How old are you? (vee alt bist doo)

20. Was kostet das? - How much does it cost? (vas kostet das)

21. Wo ist der Bahnhof? - Where is the train station? (vo ist dehr bahnhof)

22. Wo ist das Hotel? - Where is the hotel? (vo ist das ho-tell)

23. Das ist lecker. - This is delicious. (das ist leh-ker)

24. Ich habe Hunger. - I'm hungry. (ikh ha-buh hoon-ger)

25. Kann ich bitte die Speisekarte haben? - Can I have the menu please? (kahn ikh bit-teh dee shpy-ze-kahr-teh hah-ben)

26. Was empfehlen Sie? - What do you recommend? (vas emp-feh-len zee)

27. Prost! - Cheers! (prohst)

28. Guten Appetit! - Enjoy your meal! (goo-ten ap-peh-teet)

29. Wo ist die nächste U-Bahn-Station? - Where is the nearest subway station? (vo ist dee nehste oo-bahn shta-tsee-ohn)

30. Wo ist der nächste Geldautomat? - Where is the nearest ATM? (vo ist dehr nehste gel-dah-toh-maht)

31. Wo ist der nächste Supermarkt? - Where is the nearest supermarket? (vo ist dehr nehste soo-per-markt)

32. Wie komme ich zum Flughafen? - How do I get to the airport? (vee kom-meh ikh tsoom floog-hah-fen)

33. Können Sie mir helfen? - Can you help me? (kœ-nen zee mir hel-fen)

34. Ich bin verloren. - I am lost. (ikh bin ver-lo-ren)

35. Wo kann ich ein Taxi finden? - Where can I find a taxi? (vo kahn ikh ighn taks-ee fin-den)

36. Gibt es hier ein Restaurant? - Is there a restaurant around here? (gibt es heer ighn resh-to-rant)

37. Wie weit ist es zum Zentrum? - How far is it to the city center? (vee vyt ist es tsoom tsehn-troom)

38. Wie viel kostet eine Fahrkarte? - How much does a ticket cost? (vee feel kostet o iy-ne fahr-kahr-teh)

39. Darf ich bitte zahlen? - Can I pay please? (darf ikh bit-teh zah-len)

40. Wo kann ich WLAN finden? - Where can I find Wi-Fi? (vo kahn ikh vee-lahn fin-den)

41. Wie heißt das auf Deutsch? - What's that called in German? (vee heyst das owf doytsh)

42. Wo finde ich einen Geldwechsler? - Where can I find a currency exchange? (vo fin-de ikh ayn-en gelts-veysh-ler)

43. Wie viel kostet ein Bier? - How much does a beer cost? (vee feel kostet ayn beer)

44. Wie lange dauert es? - How long does it take? (vee lahng-eh dow-ert es)

45. Gibt es einen Arzt in der Nähe? - Is there a doctor nearby? (gibt es ayn-en artst in dehr neh-e)

46. Ich habe mich verlaufen. - I'm lost. (ikh ha-buh mikh fer-law-fen)

47. Ich brauche einen Dolmetscher. - I need an interpreter. (ikh brow-khe ayn-en dol-met-sher)

48. Wo ist der nächste Geldwechsler? - Where is the nearest currency exchange? (vo ist dehr neh-ste gelts-vaysh-ler)

49. Was ist das? - What is that? (vas ist das)

50. Wie spät ist die letzte Bahn? - What time is the last train? (vee shpayt ist dee let-steh bahn)

51. Wo kann ich ein Fahrrad mieten? - Where can I rent a bicycle? (vo kahn ikh ighn fahr-rad mee-ten)

52. Wo ist der nächste Bankautomat? - Where is the nearest bank ATM? (vo ist dehr nehste bank-ah-toh-maht)

53. Wie viel kostet eine Übernachtung? - How much does a night's stay cost? (vee feel kostet ayn-eh oo-ber-nakht-oong)

54. Wo ist das nächste Krankenhaus? - Where is the nearest hospital? (vo ist das nehste krang-keh-on-hawz)

55. Wie lange dauert die Fahrt? - How long does the journey take? (vee lahng-eh dow-ert dee fart)

56. Entschuldigen Sie, wo ist der Ausgang? - Excuse me, where is the exit? (ent-shool-di-gen zee, vo ist dehr auz-gang)

57. Wie geht es dir? - How are you? (vee geht es deer)

58. Wo kann ich ein Hotelzimmer buchen? - Where can I book a hotel room? (vo kahn ikh ighn ho-tell-tsim-mer boo-khen)

59. Was ist deine Lieblingsfarbe? - What is your favorite color? (vas ist dye-neh leeb-ling-far-beh)

60. Wie viel kostet das Ticket? - How much does the ticket cost? (vee feel kostet das ti-ket)

61. Wo kann ich ein Auto mieten? - Where can I rent a car? (vo kahn ikh ighn ow-to mee-ten)

62. Wo ist der nächste Geldautomat? - Where is the nearest cash machine? (vo ist dehr neh-ste gelt-au-to-mat)

63. Wie war dein Tag? - How was your day? (vee var dye-ner tag)

64. Was ist deine Lieblingsspeise? - What is your favorite food? (vas ist dye-ner leeb-lingsh-spy-ze)

65. Wo kann ich einen Stadtplan bekommen? - Where can I get a city map? (vo kahn ikh ighn-eye-nen shtat-plan bek-oh-men)

66. Ist hier WLAN verfügbar? - Is there Wi-Fi available here? (ist heer vee-lahn fer-fewg-bar)

67. Was machst du gerne in deiner Freizeit? - What do you like to do in your free time? (vas makhs do kra-ne in dy-ner fray-tsyt)

68. Wo kann ich Museen besuchen? - Where can I visit museums? (vo kahn ikh moo-zay-en bey-zy-khen)

69. Wie weit ist der Strand? - How far is the beach? (vee vyt ist dehr shtrend)

70. Hast du Haustiere? - Do you have pets? (hast doo hows-tee-reh)

71. Wo kann ich Postkarten kaufen? - Where can I buy postcards? (vo kahn ikh post-kahr-ten kow-fen)

72. Wie viel kostet eine Zugfahrkarte? - How much does a train ticket cost? (vee feel kostet ai-ne tsug-fahr-kahr-teh)

73. Wo ist die nächste Bushaltestelle? - Where is the nearest bus stop? (vo ist dee nehste boos-hal-te-shteh-leh)

74. Wo finde ich einen Geldautomaten? - Where can I find an ATM? (vo finde ikh ayn-en gel-au-to-mat-en)

75. Was isst du gerne zum Frühstück? - What do you like to eat for breakfast? (vas ist doo kra-ne tsoom fru-styk)

USEFUL BUSINESS PHRASES IN GERMAN

1. Guten Morgen. - Good morning. (goo-ten mor-gen)

2. Auf Wiedersehen. - Goodbye. (auf vee-der-zey-en)

3. Danke schön. - Thank you very much. (dahn-kuh shern)

4. Bitte. - Please. (bit-teh)

5. Entschuldigung. - Excuse me. (ent-shool-di-gung)

6. Es tut mir leid. - I'm sorry. (es toot meer lite)

7. Macht nichts. - It's alright. (mahcht niks)

8. Kein Problem. - No problem. (kine problehm)

9. Vielen Dank. - Many thanks. (fee-len dahnk)

10. Das ist ein Missverständnis. - That's a misunderstanding. (das ist ain miss-fer-shtain-dis-nis)

11. Ich verstehe nicht. - I don't understand. (ikh fair-steh-eh nikht)

12. Können Sie das bitte wiederholen? - Can you please repeat that? (kœ-nen zee das bit-teh vee-der-ho-len)

14. Sprechen Sie Englisch? - Do you speak English? (shpreh-khen zee eng-lish)

15. Ich habe eine Frage. - I have a question. (ikh ha-buh ayn-eh fra-ge)

16. Darf ich etwas hinzufügen? - May I add something? (darf ikh awt-ehs hin-tsuh-fewn)

17. Das hört sich gut an. - That sounds good. (das hœrt zikh goot ahn)

18. Was ist Ihr Standpunkt? - What is your point of view? (vas ist oor shtahnt-punkt)

19. Wir müssen eine Entscheidung treffen. - We have to make a decision. (veer myoo-sen ayn-eh ent-shy-dung treh-fen)

20. Das ergibt keinen Sinn. - That doesn't make sense. (das er-git kai-nen zin)

21. Können Sie mir helfen? - Can you help me? (kœ-nen zee meer hel-fen)

22. Ich möchte eine Bestellung aufgeben. - I would like to place an order. (ikh merkh-to ayn-eh beshtel-lung owf-gey-ben)

23. Wie viel kostet das? - How much does it cost? (vee feel kostet das)

24. Darf ich das nächste Thema ansprechen? - May I address the next topic? (darf ikh das neh-ste tay-mah ahn-shpreh-khen)

25. Wir benötigen weitere Informationen. - We need more information. (veer ben-øt-ti-gen vy-ter-eh in-fo-rmah-tsi-ohn-en)

26. Lassen Sie uns eine Lösung finden. - Let's find a solution. (lah-sen zee oons ayn-eh lew-zung fin-den)

27. Wir müssen unsere Ziele erreichen. - We need to achieve our goals. (veer myoo-sen ow-reh tsie-le eh-rey-chen)

28. Das ist unser Hauptfokus. - That is our main focus. (das ist oons-er howpt-fo-kus)

29. Ich habe Bedenken wegen... - I have concerns about... (ikh ha-buh beh-den-ken veh-gen)

30. Können wir das in einer Besprechung klären? - Can we discuss this in a meeting? (kœ-nen veer das in ayn-er be-spreh-kung kla-ren)

31. Ich stimme Ihnen zu. - I agree with you. (ikh shtim-me ee-nen tsoo)

32. Das ist nicht umsetzbar. - That's not feasible. (das ist nikht oom-sets-bar)

33. Das ist eine großartige Idee. - That's a great idea. (das ist ayn-eh grohs-ar-tee-ge ee-deh)

34. Können Sie mir bitte eine E-Mail schicken? - Can you please send me an email? (kœ-nen zee meer bit-teh ayn-eh ey-mail shi-ken)

35. Wir müssen unsere Effizienz steigern. - We need to increase our efficiency. (veer myoo-sen ow-reh ef-fi-tsi-ents shty-gern)

36. Ich würde gerne mehr darüber erfahren. - I would like to learn more about it. (ikh voo-dr-eh gehr-ne mair dah-oo-ber erfahr-en)

37. Das können wir optimieren. - We can optimize that. (das kœ-nen veer op-tee-mee-ren)

38. Haben Sie weitere Fragen? - Do you have any further questions? (hah-ben zee vy-ter-eh fra-ge-en)

39. Wir müssen das Projekt abschließen. - We need to finish the project. (veer myoo-sen das proy-ekt apsh-lee-sen)

40. Das ist eine gute Gelegenheit. - This is a good opportunity. (das ist ayn-eh goot-eh gay-le-gen-hyt)

41. Hatten Sie eine Gelegenheit, es zu überprüfen? - Did you have a chance to review it? (hat-ten zee ayn-eh gay-le-gen-hayt, es tsoo o-ber-prue-fen)

42. Das ist nicht akzeptabel. - That is not acceptable. (das ist nikht ak-sep-ta-bel)

43. Wir müssen die Deadline einhalten. - We need to meet the deadline. (veer myoo-sen dee dehdt-ly-neh yn-hal-ten)

44. Das ist ein erfolgreiches Projekt. - This is a successful project. (das ist ayn ery-fool-grees-es proy-ekt)

45. Ich möchte Verbesserungen vorschlagen. - I would like to suggest improvements. (ikh merkh-te fer-be-sser-oong-en for-shlah-gen)

46. Das ist unsere Priorität. - That is our priority. (das ist oons-er pree-yo-ree-taht)

47. Wir müssen unsere Verkaufszahlen steigern. - We need to increase our sales figures. (veer myoo-sen ow-reh fer-kowfs-tsal-en shty-gern)

48. Das ist ein wichtiges Thema. - This is an important issue. (das ist ayn vikt-iges tay-mah)

49. Wir müssen diese Herausforderung meistern. - We need to overcome this challenge. (veer myoo-sen dee-ze heh-raus-foord-er-ong my-stern)

50. Haben Sie weitere Informationen dazu? - Do you have further information about that? (hah-ben zee vy-ter-eh in-fo-rmah-tsi-ohn-en dazoo)

51. Das ist unsere Zielsetzung. - That is our objective. (das ist oons-er tsee-ehl-zeht-soong)

52. Wir müssen unsere Kunden zufriedenstellen. - We must satisfy our customers. (veer myoo-sen oons-er koon-den tsoo-freed-en-stel-len)

53. Das ist ein interessantes Projekt. - This is an interesting project. (das ist ayn in-ter-es-san-tes proy-ekt)

54. Wir müssen effektive Lösungen finden. - We need to find effective solutions. (veer myoo-sen ef-fek-tee-ve lew-zoon-en fin-den)

55. Das ist eine gute Geschäftsmöglichkeit. - This is a good business opportunity. (das ist ayn goot-e geh-shaefts-maen-likh-kait)

USEFUL POSTAL PHRASES IN GERMAN

1. Guten Tag. - Good day. (goo-ten tahk)
2. Willkommen. - Welcome. (vil-koh-men)
3. Was kann ich für Sie tun? - What can I do for you? (vas kann ikh fur zee toon)
4. Wie kann ich Ihnen helfen? - How can I help you? (vee kann ikh ee-nen hel-fen)
5. Ich möchte diesen Brief versenden. - I would like to send this letter. (ikh mehrkh-te dee-zen brief fer-zen-den)
6. Ich hätte gerne eine Briefmarke. - I would like to have a stamp. (ikh het-te gehr-ne ayn-eh breef-mar-keh)
7. Wie viel kostet der Versand? - How much does the shipping cost? (vee feel kostet der fer-zahnt)
8. Gibt es eine Tracking-Nummer? - Is there a tracking number? (gibt es ayn-eh tracking-noo-mer)
9. Wann wird das Paket zugestellt? - When will the package be delivered? (vahn vird das pa-ket tsoo-ge-shtellt)
10. Kann ich eine Quittung bekommen? - Can I get a receipt? (kann ikh ayn-eh kvee-toont be-kohm-men)
11. Wo kann ich das Paket abholen? - Where can I pick up the package? (vo kann ik das pa-ket ap-hol-en)

12. Ich möchte einen Einschreibebrief verschicken. - I would like to send a registered letter. (ikh merkh-te ayn-en yn-shry-beh-brief fer-shik-en)

13. Ich brauche eine leere Versandtasche. - I need an empty shipping envelope. (ikh brow-khe ayn-eh leh-reh fer-zahnt-tah-shuh)

14. Das Paket ist beschädigt angekommen. - The package arrived damaged. (das pa-ket ist be-shay-digt an-geh-kom-men)

15. Wann wird das Paket voraussichtlich geliefert? - When is the package expected to be delivered? (vahn vird das pa-ket fo-raus-ziht-likh guh-lie-fert)

16. Ich möchte eine Expresslieferung. - I would like an express delivery. (ikh merkh-te ayn-eh eks-press-lee-fer-oong)

17. Können Sie mir helfen, dieses Formular auszufüllen? - Can you help me fill out this form? (kœ-nen zee meer hel-fen, dee-zehs for-moo-lar oos-tsoo-few-len)

18. Ist eine Unterschrift erforderlich? - Is a signature required? (ist ayn-eh oon-tershrift er-for-der-likh)

19. Die Sendung ist verloren gegangen. - The shipment is lost. (dee zhen-doong ist fer-lo-ren ge-gang-en)

20. Kann ich das Porto online bezahlen? - Can I pay the postage online? (kann ikh das pohr-toh on-lyne be-za-len)

21. Welche Zahlungsmethoden akzeptieren Sie? - What payment methods do you accept? (vel-khe tsah-loongs-meh-to-den ak-zept-ee-ren zee)

22. Ich möchte einen Paketschein. - I would like a package label. (ikh merkh-te ayn-en pa-ket-shyn)

23. Bitte bringen Sie mich zur nächsten Postfiliale. - Please take me to the nearest post office. (bit-teh bren-gen zee mikh tsoor neh-ste post-fee-lee-ah-leh)

24. Wo kann ich einen Briefkasten finden? - Where can I find a mailbox? (vo kann ikh ayn-en breef-kas-ten fin-den)

25. Das Päckchen ist nicht angekommen. - The parcel did not arrive. (das pehk-chen ist nikht an-geh-kom-men)

26. Kann ich eine Paketverfolgungsnummer haben? - Can I have a package tracking number? (kann ikh ayn-eh pa-ket-fuhr-loog-oongs-noo-mer ha-ben)

27. Wann öffnen Sie wieder? - When do you open again? (vahn œff-nen zee vi-der)

28. Das ist das richtige Porto. - This is the correct postage. (das ist das rik-tee-ge pohr-toh)

29. Wo ist der Zoll? - Where is customs? (vo ist der tsol)

30. Das Päckchen soll bis morgen zugestellt werden. - The parcel should be delivered by tomorrow. (das pehk-chen zoll bis mor-gen tsoo-ge-shtellt ver-den)

31. Ich möchte das Paket versichern. - I would like to insure the package. (ikh merkh-te das pa-ket fer-zeern)

32. Das ist ein internationaler Versand. - This is an international shipment. (das ist ayn in-tehr-na-tsi-o-neh fer-zahnt)

33. Kann ich eine Sendungsverfolgung machen? - Can I track a shipment? (kann ikh ayn-eh zhen-doongs-fer-foolg-oong ma-khen)

34. Welcher Postdienst ist der schnellste? - Which postal service is the fastest? (vel-kher post-deenst ist der shnel-ste)

35. Wo ist das nächste Postamt? - Where is the nearest post office? (vo ist das neh-ste post-ahmt)

36. Kann ich eine Ersatzlieferung erhalten? - Can I receive a replacement delivery? (kann ikh ayn-eh er-zats-lee-fer-oong er-hal-ten)

37. Ich habe einen Nachsendeauftrag. - I have a mail forwarding request. (ikh ha-buh ayn-en nahk-sen-deh-owf-traht)

38. Das ist der Empfängername. - This is the recipient's name. (das ist der emf-fen-er-na-meh)

39. Wann wird der Brief zugestellt? - When will the letter be delivered? (vahn vird der brief tsoo-ge-shtellt)

40. Es gab ein Missverständnis bei der Lieferung. - There was a misunderstanding with the delivery. (es gab ayn miss-fer-shtain-dis-nis bi der lee-fe-rung)

41. Das Paket wurde zur Abholung hinterlassen. - The package was left for pick-up. (das pa-ket vur-de tsur ap-ho-lung hin-ter-lassen)

42. Kann ich einen Expresskurier rufen? - Can I call an express courier? (kann ikh ayn-en eks-press-ku-ree-er roo-fen)

43. Das ist die Absenderadresse. - This is the sender's address. (das ist dee ab-sen-der-ah-dres-se)

44. Ich möchte eine Einschreibenummer haben. - I would like to have a registered number. (ikh merkh-te ayn-eh yn-shry-ben-oom-mer ha-ben)

45. Der Brief wurde falsch zugestellt. - The letter was delivered incorrectly. (der brief vur-de falsht tsoo-ge-shtellt)

46. Wie lange dauert die Lieferung? - How long does the delivery take? (vee lan-ge dou-ert dee lee-fe-rung)

47. Das Paket muss zurückgeschickt werden. - The package needs to be returned. (das pa-ket moos tsuruek-ge-shikt ver-den)

48. Wie kann ich eine Nachnahme-Zahlung leisten? - How can I make a cash on delivery payment? (vee kann ikh ayn-eh nahk-nah-me-tsah-loong li-sten)

49. Wo ist der Briefkastenschlitz? - Where is the letterbox slot? (vo ist der breef-kas-ten-shleets)

50. Kann ich einen Karton kaufen? - Can I buy a box? (kann ikh ayn-en kar-ton cow-fen)

51. Der Brief ist verloren gegangen. - The letter is lost. (der brief ist fer-loh-ren ge-gang-en)

52. Dürfen Sie das Paket öffnen? - Are you allowed to open the package? (door-fen zee das pa-ket œf-nen)

53. Das Paket ist nicht rechtzeitig angekommen. - The package did not arrive on time. (das pa-ket ist nikht rikht-ti-g ar-ghe-kom-men

54. Kann ich eine Versandbestätigung erhalten? - Can I get a shipping confirmation? (kann ikh ayn-eh fer-zahnt-be-shte-ti-gung er-hal-ten)

55. Wie viel wiegt das Paket? - How much does the package weigh? (vee feel veegt das pa-ket)

56. Die Lieferung hat sich verzögert. - The delivery is delayed. (dee lee-fe-rung hat zikh fer-tsœ-gert)

57. Können Sie das an eine andere Adresse senden? - Can you send it to a different address? (kœ-nen zee das an ayn-eh an-dere-ah-dres-se shi-ken)

58. Das Paket wurde beschädigt. - The package was damaged. (das pa-ket vur-de be-shay-digt)

59. Wie lange dauert der internationale Versand? - How long does international shipping take? (vee lan-ge dou-ert der in-tehr-na-tsi-o-na-le fer-zahnt)

USEFUL AIRPORT PHRASES IN GERMAN

1. Guten Tag. - Good day. (goo-ten tahk)
2. Willkommen. - Welcome. (vil-koh-men)
3. Wo ist der Flughafen? - Where is the airport? (vo ist der floo-ha-fen)
4. Wie komme ich zur Gepäckausgabe? - How do I get to the baggage claim area? (vee kom-me ikh tsoor geh-pehk-owg-za-ghe)
5. Wo ist der Ausgang? - Where is the exit? (vo ist der owz-gang)
6. Ist mein Flug pünktlich? - Is my flight on time? (ist myn floog pœnkt-likh)
7. Wo ist das Terminal? - Where is the terminal? (vo ist das ter-mee-nal)
8. Ich habe meinen Pass verloren. - I have lost my passport. (ikh ha-bey myn-en pahs fer-lo-ren)
9. Wo ist der Check-in-Schalter? - Where is the check-in counter? (vo ist der chek-in-shal-ter)
10. Sprechen Sie Englisch? - Do you speak English? (shpre-khen zee en-glish)
11. Kann ich meinen Sitzplatz wählen? - Can I choose my seat? (kann ikh my-nen sits-plats vah-len)
12. Wie lange dauert der Flug? - How long does the flight take? (vee lan-ge dou-ert der floog)

13. Wo kann ich meinen Koffer abholen? - Where can I pick up my suitcase? (vo kann ikh my-nen ko-fer ap-hol-en)

14. Wo ist die Sicherheitskontrolle? - Where is the security checkpoint? (vo ist dee zi-cher-haits-kon-trol-le)

15. Ist es erlaubt, Flüssigkeiten im Handgepäck mitzunehmen? - Is it allowed to carry liquids in hand luggage? (ist es er-lahbt, floes-si-gkhai-ten im hant-geh-pehk mit-tsoo-ne-men)

16. Wann sollte ich am Gate sein? - When should I be at the gate? (vahn zœl-te ikh am geyt zine)

17. Wo ist die Zollkontrolle? - Where is customs control? (vo ist dee tsol-kon-trol-le)

18. Kann ich eine Steckdose finden? - Can I find a power outlet? (kann ikh ayn-eh shtek-do-ze fin-den)

19. Wie viel kostet das Parken? - How much does parking cost? (vee feel kostet das par-ken)

20. Ist WLAN verfügbar? - Is Wi-Fi available? (ist vee-lahn fer-foo-gbar)

21. Wo ist das Informationsschalter? - Where is the information desk? (vo ist das in-for-ma-tsi-ons-shal-ter)

22. Kann ich hier rauchen? - Can I smoke here? (kann ikh heer rou-khen)

23. Wo kann ich Geld wechseln? - Where can I exchange money? (vo kann ikh ghelt vek-seln)

24. Kann ich einen Mietwagen buchen? - Can I book a rental car? (kann ikh ayn-en meet-va-gen boo-khen)

25. Gibt es einen Geldautomaten? - Is there an ATM? (gibt es ayn-en ghelt-ow-to-ma-ten)

26. Wo ist der Abflugbereich? - Where is the departure area? (vo ist der ab-floog-be-raykh)

27. Wo ist die Toilette? - Where is the restroom? (vo ist dee toa-let-te)

28. Wie lange dauert die Passkontrolle? - How long does passport control take? (vee lan-ge dou-ert dee pahs-kon-trol-le)

29. Kann ich eine Fahrkarte kaufen? - Can I buy a ticket? (kann ikh ayn-eh fahr-kahr-te cow-fen)

30. Wann kommt mein Flug an? - When does my flight arrive? (vahn komt myn floog ahn)

31. Gibt es einen Aufzug? - Is there an elevator? (gibt es ayn-en ow-foopt)

32. Wo ist die Gepäckaufbewahrung? - Where is the luggage storage? (vo ist dee geh-pehk-owf-be-va-rung)

33. Wo sind die Abflugtafeln? - Where are the departure boards? (vo zind dee ab-floog-ta-feln)

34. Kann ich meinen Sitzplatz ändern? - Can I change my seat? (kann ikh my-nen sits-plats ern-dern)

35. Wo ist die Einreisekontrolle? - Where is the immigration control? (vo ist dee yn-ry-ze-kon-trol-le)

36. Wie komme ich zur Bahnstation? - How do I get to the train station? (vee kom-me ikh tsoor bahn-sta-tsee-on)

37. Wo ist die Passkontrollstelle? - Where is the passport control point? (vo ist dee pahs-kon-trol-shtel-le)

38. Kann ich meinen Flug umbuchen? - Can I reschedule my flight? (kann ikh my-nen floog oom-boo-khen)

39. Wo sind die Gepäckwagen? - Where are the luggage carts? (vo zind dee geh-pehk-va-ghen)

40. Gibt es kostenlose Parkplätze? - Are there free parking spaces? (gibt es kos-ten-lo-zeh park-pla-tseh)

41. Wie komme ich zur Bushaltestelle? - How do I get to the bus stop? (vee kom-me ikh tsoor boos-hal-te-stel-le)

42. Wo ist die Zollabfertigung? - Where is customs clearance? (vo ist dee tsol-apf-ehr-ti-gung)

43. Kann ich hier mein Handy aufladen? - Can I charge my phone here? (kann ikh heer myn hen-dey ow-flah-den)

44. Wo kann ich einen Kaffee trinken? - Where can I have a coffee? (vo kann ikh ayn-en kaf-fay trin-ken)

45. Wie spät ist die letzte Sicherheitskontrolle? - What time is the last security check? (vee shpet ist dee letst-eh zi-cher-haits-kon-trol-le)

46. Wo ist der Weg zum Mietwagenschalter? - Where is the way to the car rental counter? (vo ist der vek tsoom meet-va-gen-shal-ter)

47. Wo ist der Check-out-Schalter? - Where is the check-out counter? (vo ist der chek-owt-shal-ter)

48. Kann ich hier etwas essen? - Can I eat something here? (kann ikh heer et-vas es-sen)

49. Wo kann ich Duty-Free-Einkäufe machen? - Where can I do duty-free shopping? (vo kann ikh doo-tee-free-ayn-koy-fe ma-khen)

50. Wie komme ich zur Mietwagenrückgabe? - How do I get to the car rental return? (vee kom-me ikh tsoor meet-va-gen-rikhg-abe)

Numbers in German

1 - eins (ayns)
2 - zwei (tsvahy)
3 - drei (dry)
4 - vier (feer)
5 - fünf (fynf)
6 - sechs (zeks)
7 - sieben (zeeben)
8 - acht (akt)
9 - neun (noyn)
10 - zehn (tsayn)
11 - elf (elf)
12 - zwölf (tsoolf)
13 - dreizehn (dry-tsayn)
14 - vierzehn (feer-tsayn)
15 - fünfzehn (fynf-tsayn)
16 - sechzehn (zeks-tsayn)
17 - siebzehn (zeeb-tsayn)
18 - achtzehn (akht-tsayn)
19 - neunzehn (noyn-tsayn)
20 - zwanzig (tsvan-tsik)
21 - einundzwanzig (ayn-oont-ts-van-tsik)

22 - zweiundzwanzig (tsvay-oont-ts-van-tsik)

...

99 - neunundneunzig (noyn-oont-noyn-tsikh)

100 - einhundert (ayn-hoon-dert)

USEFUL HOLIDAY PHRASES IN GERMAN

1. Frohe Feiertage! (Froh-uh Fay-er-tah-geh) - Happy holidays!

2. Fröhliche Weihnachten! (Frur-lick-uh Vye-nahk-ten) - Merry Christmas!

3. Alles Gute zum neuen Jahr! (Al-les Goo-teh tsoom noy-en yahr) - Happy New Year!

4. Frohes Fest! (Froh-es Fest) - Happy celebration!

5. Schöne Ferien! (Schur-nuh Feh-ree-en) - Have a great vacation!

6. Guten Rutsch ins neue Jahr! (Goo-ten Rootsh ins noy-en yahr) - Happy New Year's Eve!

7. Ich wünsche dir eine besinnliche Zeit. (Eekh woon-she deer I-ne beh-zin-lick-uh Tsyt) - I wish you a peaceful time.

8. Genieße die Feiertage! (Geh-nee-ay dee Fay-er-tah-geh) - Enjoy the holidays!

9. Ein frohes neues Jahr! (Ay-n froh-es noy-es yahr) - Happy New Year!

10. Viel Glück im neuen Jahr! (Feel Glook eem noy-en yahr) - Good luck in the New Year!

11. Ich hoffe, du hast eine tolle Zeit. (Eekh hof-uh, doo hast I-ne toh-luh Tsyt) - I hope you have a great time.

12. Das Fest der Liebe. (Dahs Fest dare Lee-buh) - The festival of love.

13. Bist du bereit für die Feiertage? (Beest doo beh-rait fur dee Fay-er-tah-geh) - Are you ready for the holidays?

14. Lass uns das Neue Jahr feiern! (Lahs oons dahs Noy-es yahr fy-ern) - Let's celebrate the New Year!

15. Ich wünsche dir ein frohes Weihnachtsfest. (Eekh woon-she deer ayn froh-es Vye-nahkts-fest) - I wish you a Merry Christmas.

16. Prost Neujahr! (Prohst Noy-yahr) - Cheers to the New Year!

17. Was sind deine Pläne für die Ferien? (Vahs zint dee-neh Plah-ne fur dee Feh-ree-en) - What are your plans for the holidays?

18. Ich hoffe, du bekommst alles, was du dir wünschst. (Eekh hof-uh, doo buh-komst ayl-les, vahs doo deer woon-schst) - I hope you get everything you wish for.

19. Ich freue mich darauf, Zeit mit meiner Familie zu verbringen. (Eekh froy-uh mikh dah-roof, Tsyt meet my-ner Fah-mee-lee tsoo fair-breen-gen) - I'm looking forward to spending time with my family.

20. Wünsche euch allen ein schönes Fest! (Voon-she oykh al-len ayn shur-nes Fest) - Wishing you all a lovely celebration!

21. Hab eine tolle Zeit! (Hahb I-ne toh-luh Tsyt) - Have a great time!

22. Ich hoffe, du genießt die Feiertage in vollen Zügen. (Eekh hof-uh, doo geh-nee-est dee Fay-er-tah-geh in fohl-en Tsukh-en) - I hope you enjoy the holidays to the fullest.

23. Frohes neues Jahr! Viel Erfolg und Gesundheit! (Froh-es noy-es yahr! Feel air-folgh oont Geh-zoon-dhayt) - Happy New Year! Much success and good health!

24. Frohe Weihnachten und ein glückliches neues Jahr! (Froh-uh Vye-nahk-ten oont ayn glook-likh-es noy-es yahr) - Merry Christmas and a happy New Year!

25. Ich wünsche dir einen besinnlichen Heiligabend. (Eekh woon-she deer I-nen beh-zin-lick-en Hay-likh-ah-bent) - I wish you a peaceful Christmas Eve.

26. Einen guten Start ins neue Jahr! (Ay-nen goo-ten Shtart ins noy-en yahr) - A good start to the New Year!

27. Wünsche dir und deiner Familie frohe Feiertage. (Voon-she deer oont dy-ner Fah-mee-lee froh-uh Fay-er-tah-geh) - Wishing you and your family happy holidays.

28. Hab ein frohes Fest! (Hahb ayn froh-es Fest) - Have a merry celebration!

29. Frohe Festtage und einen guten Rutsch ins neue Jahr! (Froh-uh Fest-tah-geh oont ay-nen goo-ten Rootsh ins noy-en yahr) - Happy celebrations and a happy New Year's Eve!

30. Ich wünsche dir einen guten Rutsch ins neue Jahr! (Eekh woon-she deer I-nen goo-ten Rootsh ins noy-en yahr) - I wish you a happy New Year's Eve!

31. Lass uns das Jahr in Freude beenden! (Lahs oons dahs yahr in Froy-duh bay-en-den) - Let's end the year with joy!

32. Wünsche euch eine erholsame Zeit! (Voon-she oykh I-ne air-hol-zah-me Tsyt) - Wishing you a restful time!

33. Ich hoffe, du hast eine entspannte Pause. (Eekh hof-uh, doo hast I-ne ent-shpant-teh Pow-zuh) - I hope you have a relaxing break.

34. Fröhliche Feiertage und einen guten Start ins neue Jahr! (Frur-lick-uh Fay-er-tah-geh oont ay-nen goo-ten Shtart ins noy-en yahr) - Merry holidays and a good start to the New Year!

35. Habt eine schöne Zeit zusammen! (Hahbt I-ne shur-neh Tsyt tsoo-zahm-en) - Have a lovely time together!

36. Ein wunderbares Weihnachtsfest und alles Gute für das kommende Jahr! (Ayn voon-der-bah-res Vye-nahkts-fest oont al-les Goo-teh fur dahs koh-men-dee yahr) - A wonderful Christmas and all the best for the coming year!

37. Ich hoffe, du kommst gut ins neue Jahr! (Eekh hof-uh, doo kohmst goot ins noy-en yahr) - I hope you have a good start to the New Year!

38. Wünsche dir viel Freude und Glück! (Voon-she deer feel Froy-duh oont Glook) - Wishing you much joy and happiness!

39. Frohes Fest und einen guten Rutsch! (Froh-es Fest oont ay-nen goo-ten Rootsh) - Happy celebration and a good slide (into the New Year)!

40. Ich hoffe, du hast eine fantastische Auszeit. (Eekh hof-uh, doo hast I-ne fan-tas-tish-uh Ow-saits) - I hope you have a fantastic time off.

41. Prost auf ein erfolgreiches neues Jahr! (Prohst owp ayn air-fol-grikh-es noy-es yahr) - Cheers to a successful New Year!

42. Wünsche dir einen schönen Urlaub! (Voon-she deer I-nen shur-nen Oor-laub) - Wishing you a wonderful vacation!

43. Frohes Weihnachtsfest und einen guten Rutsch! (Froh-es Vye-nahkts-fest oont ay-nen goo-ten Rootsh) - Merry Christmas and a good slide!

44. Ich wünsche dir Spaß und Entspannung. (Eekh woon-she deer shpahss oont Ent-shpahn-oong) - I wish you fun and relaxation.

45. Habt eine fröhliche und besinnliche Zeit! (Hahbt I-ne Frur-lick-uh oont beh-zin-lick-uh Tsyt) - Have a merry and peaceful time!

46. Genießt die Weihnachtszeit! (Geh-nee-est dee Vye-nahkts-tsyt) - Enjoy the Christmas season!

47. Frohes neues Jahr voller Freude! (Froh-es noy-es yahr fohl-er Froy-duh) - Happy New Year full of joy!

48. Lass uns das Jahr mit einem Knall beenden! (Lahs oons dahs yahr mit AY-nem knall bay-en-den) - Let's end the year with a bang!

49. Wünsche dir einen guten Rutsch ins neue Jahr voller Erfolg! (Voon-she deer I-nen goo-ten Rootsh ins noy-en yahr fohl-er air-folg) - Wishing you a happy New Year full of success!

50. Frohe Festtage und einen guten Start ins neue Jahr! (Froh-uh Fest-tah-geh oont ay-nen goo-ten Shtart ins noy-en yahr) - Happy celebrations and a good start to the New Year!

51. Habt eine wundervolle Zeit miteinander! (Hahbt I-ne voon-der-vohl-uh Tsyt mit-eye-nan-der) - Have a wonderful time together!

52. Genießt die Weihnachtsferien! (Geh-nee-est dee Vye-nahkts-feh-ree-en) - Enjoy the Christmas holidays!

53. Ein erfolgreiches neues Jahr! (Ayn air-fol-grikh-es noy-es yahr) - A successful New Year!

54. Ich wünsche dir eine frohe und besinnliche Weihnachtszeit. (Eekh woon-she deer I-ne froh-uh oont beh-zin-lick-uh Vye-nahkts-tsyt) - I wish you a merry and peaceful Christmas season.

55. Habt eine traumhafte Zeit! (Hahbt I-ne troum-hahf-te Tsyt) - Have a dreamy time!

56. Frohe Feiertage und einen guten Rutsch ins neue Jahr! (Froh-uh Fay-er-tah-geh oont ay-nen goo-ten Rootsh ins noy-en yahr) - Happy holidays and a good slide into the New Year!

57. Lass uns das Jahr mit Freude verabschieden! (Lahs oons dahs yahr mit Froy-duh feh-rap-shee-den) - Let's bid farewell to the year with joy!

58. Wünsche dir einen schönen Winterurlaub! (Voon-she deer I-nen shur-nen Vin-ter-oor-laub) - Wishing you a lovely winter vacation!

59. Fröhliche Weihnachtszeit und einen guten Rutsch ins neue Jahr! (Frur-lick-uh Vye-nahkts-tsyt oont ay-nen goo-ten Rootsh ins noy-en yahr) - Merry Christmas season and a good slide into the New Year!

60. Ich wünsche dir eine erholsame Auszeit. (Eekh woon-she deer I-ne air-hol-zah-me Ow-saits) - I wish you a relaxing time off.

61. Prosit Neujahr! (Proh-zeet Noy-yahr) - Cheers to the New Year!

62. Frohe Festtage und einen guten Rutsch ins neue Jahr! (Froh-uh Fest-tah-geh oont ay-nen goo-ten Rootsh ins noy-en yahr) - Happy celebrations and a good slide into the New Year!

63. Grüße aus dem Urlaub! (Groo-uhss ows dem Oor-laub) - Greetings from vacation!

64. Frohe Weihnachten und ein gesundes neues Jahr! (Froh-uh Vye-nahk-ten oont ayn ge-zoon-des noy-es yahr) - Merry Christmas and a healthy New Year!

65. Ich wünsche dir eine unvergessliche Zeit. (Eekh woon-she deer I-ne oon-ver-ges-likh-uh Tsyt) - I wish you an unforgettable time.

66. Habt eine fantastische Zeit zusammen! (Hahbt I-ne fan-tas-tish-uh Tsyt tsoo-zahm-en) - Have a fantastic time together!

67. Ein frohes und besinnliches Weihnachtsfest! (Ayn froh-es oont beh-zin-lick-es Vye-nahkts-fest) - A merry and peaceful Christmas!

68. Ich hoffe, du hast viel Spaß. (Eekh hof-uh, doo hast feel shpahss) - I hope you have lots of fun.

69. Schöne Weihnachten und ein erfülltes neues Jahr! (Shur-neh Vye-nahkts-en oont ayn air-fool-tess noy-es yahr) - Merry Christmas and a fulfilling New Year!

70. Habt eine frohe und gesegnete Zeit! (Hahbt I-ne froh-uh oont ge-zeg-nete Tsyt) - Have a joyful and blessed time!

71. Das war ein tolles Jahr! (Dahs var ayn toh-les yahr) - That was a great year!

72. Frohe Festtage und einen guten Rutsch ins neue Jahr! (Froh-uh Fest-tah-geh oont ay-nen goo-ten Rootsh ins noy-en yahr) - Happy celebrations and a good slide into the New Year!

73. Wünsche dir einen angenehmen Urlaub! (Voon-she deer I-nen ang-eh-nay-men Oor-laub) - Wishing you a pleasant vacation!

USEFUL TELEPHONE PHRASES IN GERMAN

1. Guten Tag! (Goo-ten Tahk) - Good day!

2. Hallo! (Hah-loh) - Hello!

3. Wie kann ich Ihnen helfen? (Vee kahn eekh ee-nen hel-fen) - How can I help you?

4. Ich möchte jemanden sprechen. (Eekh mehrk-teh yeh-man-den shpre-khen) - I would like to speak to someone.

5. Könnten Sie mich bitte mit... verbinden? (Kuhn-ten zee mik bitt-uh mit... fair-bind-en) - Could you please connect me to...?

6. Ist... da? (Ist... dah) - Is... there?

7. Einen Moment, bitte. (Ay-nen Mo-mennt, bitt-uh) - One moment, please.

8. Warten Sie einen Augenblick. (Vahr-ten zee ay-nen ow-gen-blick) - Please wait a moment.

9. Ich rufe an, um... zu fragen. (Eekh roo-fuh ahn, oom... tsoo frah-gen) - I'm calling to ask about...

10. Können Sie mir mehr Informationen geben? (Kuhn-nen zee meer in-fohr-mah-tsee-ohn-en gay-ben) - Can you give me more information?

11. Könnten Sie das bitte wiederholen? (Kuhn-ten zee dahs bitt-uh vee-dehr-hoh-len) - Could you please repeat that?

12. Entschuldigen Sie, ich habe Sie nicht richtig verstanden. (Ent-shool-dee-gen zee, eekh hah-buh zee nisht rikh-tikh fair-shtan-den) - Excuse me, I didn't understand you correctly.

13. Verbinden Sie mich bitte mit der Abteilung für... (Fair-bind-en zee mik bitt-uh mit dare Ab-til-oong fur...) - Please connect me to the department for...

14. Mein Name ist... (Mine Nah-me ist...) - My name is...

15. Kann ich eine Nachricht hinterlassen? (Kahn eekh oyn-e nah-shrikt hin-tuhr-lassen) - Can I leave a message?

16. Wann kann ich zurückrufen? (Vahn kahn eekh tsuh-ruek-roo-fen) - When can I call back?

17. Vielen Dank für Ihre Hilfe. (Fee-len Dank fur ee-re Hil-fuh) - Thank you very much for your help.

18. Das war alles. (Dahs var al-les) - That's all.

19. Auf Wiederhören! (Owf Vee-der-ho-ren) - Goodbye! (on the phone)

20. Ich wünsche Ihnen einen schönen Tag. (Eekh woon-she ee-nen shur-nen Tahk) - I wish you a nice day

USEFUL WEATHER PHRASES IN GERMAN

1. Wie ist das Wetter heute? - How is the weather today?
2. Es ist sonnig. - It's sunny.
3. Es ist bewölkt. - It's cloudy.
4. Es regnet. - It's raining.
5. Es schneit. - It's snowing.
6. Es ist windig. - It's windy.
7. Es ist heiß. - It's hot.
8. Es ist kalt. - It's cold.
9. Es ist neblig. - It's foggy.
10. Es blitzt und donnert. - There's lightning and thunder.
11. Der Himmel ist klar. - The sky is clear.
12. Es gibt einen Sturm. - There's a storm.
13. Es gibt leichten Nebel. - There's light fog.
14. Es gibt starke Gewitter. - There are strong thunderstorms.
15. Es gibt heftige Regenschauer. - There are heavy rain showers.
16. Es gibt leichten Schneefall. - There's light snowfall.
17. Es gibt schweren Schneefall. - There's heavy snowfall.
18. Es gibt eine Schneeböe. - There's a snow squall.
19. Die Temperatur beträgt... Grad Celsius. - The temperature is... degrees Celsius.
20. Es ist schwül. - It's humid.

21. Es ist frisch. - It's cool.
22. Es ist angenehm. - It's pleasant.
23. Es ist drückend. - It's muggy.
24. Es ist regnerisch. - It's rainy.
25. Die Sonne scheint. - The sun is shining.
26. Die Wolken ziehen auf. - The clouds are moving in.
27. Der Wind weht stark. - The wind is blowing strongly.
28. Der Himmel verdunkelt sich. - The sky is darkening.
29. Der Boden ist gefroren. - The ground is frozen.
30. Die Blätter fallen. - The leaves are falling.
31. Die Pflanzen brauchen Wasser. - The plants need water.
32. Der Schnee schmilzt. - The snow is melting.
33. Der Regenschirm ist wichtig. - The umbrella is important.
34. Der Regenbogen erscheint. - The rainbow is appearing.
35. Die Vögel zwitschern. - The birds are chirping.
36. Die Luft ist frisch. - The air is fresh.
37. Die Tage werden länger. - The days are getting longer.
38. Die Nächte werden kürzer. - The nights are getting shorter.
39. Der Frost setzt ein. - The frost is setting in.
40. Die Blumen blühen. - The flowers are blooming.
41. Die Bäume sind grün. - The trees are green.
42. Die Hitze ist unerträglich. - The heat is unbearable.
43. Die Kälte zieht in die Knochen. - The cold is bone-chilling.
44. Die Luftfeuchtigkeit ist hoch. - The humidity is high.
45. Die Luft ist klar und frisch. - The air is clear and fresh.
46. Der Morgentau liegt auf den Blättern. - The morning dew rests on the leaves.
47. Der Sommer naht. - Summer is approaching.
48. Der Herbst beginnt. - Autumn is beginning.
49. Der Winter bricht herein. - Winter is coming.

MULTILINGUAL PHRASE BOOK 175

50. Der Frühling erwacht. - Spring is awakening.

51. Es gibt Hagel. - There's hail.

52. Es gibt ein Gewitter. - There's a thunderstorm.

53. Der Wind rauscht durch die Bäume. - The wind rustles through the trees.

54. Die Sonne geht auf. - The sun rises.

55. Der See ist gefroren. - The lake is frozen.

56. Der Himmel färbt sich rot. - The sky turns red.

57. Es gibt starke Windböen. - There are strong gusts of wind.

58. Der Nebel lichtet sich. - The fog is clearing.

59. Es gibt vereinzelt Regenschauer. - There are scattered rain showers.

60. Es gibt eine Hitzewelle. - There's a heatwave.

61. Die Schneedecke taut. - The snow cover is melting.

62. Es gibt ein Tiefdruckgebiet. - There's a low-pressure area.

63. Die Luft ist stickig. - The air is stuffy.

64. Die Wolken werden dichter. - The clouds are thickening.

65. Es gibt starken Niederschlag. - There's heavy precipitation.

66. Die Temperaturen steigen. - The temperatures are rising.

67. Es gibt Böen bis zu... km/h. - There are gusts of wind up to... km/h.

68. Die Luft ist schwül und drückend. - The air is humid and heavy.

69. Es gibt eine Regenfront. - There's a rain front.

70. Die Sonne verschwindet hinter den Wolken. - The sun disappears behind the clouds.

71. Der Novembernebel liegt über dem Land. - The November fog covers the land.

72. Der Tag wird immer kürzer. - The day is getting shorter and shorter.

73. Es gibt hohe Wellen auf dem Meer. - There are high waves on the sea.

74. Das Gras ist feucht vom Tau. - The grass is damp from the dew.

75. Die Straßen sind glatt. - The roads are slippery.

76. Der Himmel ist wolkenverhangen. - The sky is overcast.

77. Der Himmel klart auf. - The sky is clearing up.

78. Es gibt viel Schnee. - There's a lot of snow.

79. Die Sonne geht unter. - The sun sets.

80. Es gibt Nebelschwaden. - There are fog patches.

81. Die Wolken ziehen schnell vorbei. - The clouds are moving quickly.

82. Es gibt leichten Hagel. - There's light hail.

83. Die Temperaturen fallen. - The temperatures are falling.

84. Es gibt anhaltenden Starkregen. - There's persistent heavy rain.

85. Es ist schwül-warm. - It's sultry.

86. Die Blätter färben sich bunt. - The leaves are changing colors.

87. Es gibt einen Wetterumschwung. - There's a change in weather.

88. Die Natur erwacht zum Leben. - Nature awakens to life.

89. Es gibt dichten Nebel. - There's thick fog.

90. Der Himmel zeigt sich grau. - The sky appears gray.

91. Der Boden ist schlammig. - The ground is muddy.

92. Die Wolkenformationen sind faszinierend. - The cloud formations are fascinating.

93. Es gibt leichten Frost. - There's light frost.

94. Die Luft ist klar und erfrischend. - The air is clear and refreshing.

95. Es gibt Nebelschwaden über den Flüssen. - There are fog patches over the rivers.

96. Der Wind lässt nach. - The wind is subsiding.

97. Es gibt ein Unwetter. - There's a severe weather.

98. Die Tage werden kühler. - The days are getting cooler.
99. Die Nächte werden länger. - The nights are getting longer.
100. Das Wetter ist wechselhaft. - The weather is changeable.

Milton Keynes UK
Ingram Content Group UK Ltd.
UKHW010200230823
427286UK00001B/37